Problem Solving, Communication, and Reasoning

Patterns and Reasoning

grade 3

Carole Greenes
Linda Schulman Dacey
Rika Spungin

Dale Seymour Publications®
White Plains, New York

This book is published by Dale Seymour Publications®,
an imprint of Addison Wesley Longman, Inc.

Dale Seymour Publications
10 Bank Street
White Plains, New York 10602
Customer Service: 800-872-1100

Managing Editor: Catherine Anderson
Senior Editor: John Nelson
Project Editor: Mali Apple
Production/Manufacturing Director: Janet Yearian
Sr. Production/Manufacturing Coordinator: Fiona Santoianni
Design Director: Phyllis Aycock
Cover and Interior Illustrations: Jared Lee
Text and Cover Design: Tracey Munz
Composition and Computer Graphics: Alan Noyes

Order number 21875
ISBN 0-7690-0017-7

1 2 3 4 5 6 7 8 9 10-ML-03 02 01 00 99

Contents

Introduction

Why Was *Hot Math Topics* Developed?

The *Hot Math Topics* series was developed for several reasons:

- to offer students practice and maintenance of previously learned skills and concepts
- to enhance problem solving and mathematical reasoning abilities
- to build literacy skills
- to nurture collaborative learning behaviors

Practicing and maintaining concepts and skills

Although textbooks and core curriculum materials do treat the topics explored in this series, their treatment is often limited by the lesson format and the page size. As a consequence, there are often not enough opportunities for students to practice newly acquired concepts and skills related to the topics, or to connect the topics to other content areas. *Hot Math Topics* provides the necessary practice and mathematical connections.

Similarly, core instructional programs often do not do a very good job of helping students maintain their skills. Although textbooks do include reviews of previously learned material, they are frequently limited to sidebars or boxed-off areas on one or two pages in each chapter, with four or five exercises in each box. Each set of problems is intended only as a sampling of previously taught topics, rather than as a complete review. In the selection and placement of the review exercises, little or no attention is given to levels of complexity of the problems. By contrast, *Hot Math Topics* targets specific topics and gives students more experience with concepts and skills related to them. The problems are sequenced by difficulty, allowing students to hone their skills. And, because they are not tied to specific lessons, the problems can be used at any time.

Enhancing problem solving and mathematical reasoning abilities

Hot Math Topics presents students with situations in which they may use a variety of problem solving strategies, including

- designing and conducting experiments to generate or collect data
- guessing, checking, and revising guesses
- organizing data in lists or tables in order to identify patterns and relationships
- choosing appropriate computational algorithms and deciding on a sequence of computations
- using inverse operations in "work backward" solution paths

For their solutions, students are also required to bring to bear various methods of reasoning, including

- deductive reasoning
- inductive reasoning
- proportional reasoning

For example, to solve clue-type problems, students must reason deductively and make inferences about mathematical relationships in order to generate candidates for the solutions and to home in on those that meet all of the problem's conditions.

To identify and continue a pattern and then write a rule for finding the next term in that pattern, students must reason inductively.

To compute equivalent ratios and make trades, students must reason proportionally.

In addition to using these reasoning methods, students must apply their number sense skills. Number sense is brought to bear when students estimate or compare magnitudes of numbers and when they must determine the type of number appropriate for a given situation.

Building communication and literacy skills

Hot Math Topics offers students opportunities to write and talk about mathematical ideas. For many problems, students must describe their solution paths, justify their solutions, give their opinions, or write or tell stories.

Some problems have multiple solution methods. With these problems, students may have to compare their methods with those of their peers and talk about how their approaches are alike and different.

Other problems have multiple solutions, requiring students to confer to be sure they have found all possible answers.

Nurturing collaborative learning behaviors

Several of the problems can be solved by students working together. Some are designed specifically as partner problems. By working collaboratively, students can develop expertise in posing questions that call for clarification or verification, brainstorming solution strategies, and following another person's line of reasoning.

What Is in *Patterns and Reasoning*?

This book contains 100 problems and tasks that focus on patterns and reasoning. The mathematics content, the mathematical connections, the problem solving strategies, and the communication skills that are emphasized are described below.

Mathematics content

Patterns and reasoning problems and tasks require students to

- continue, describe, generalize, and create patterns
- use deductive, inductive, spatial, and proportional reasoning to solve problems
- identify relationships in maps, scatter plots, and diagrams
- identify and describe similarities among elements in a group
- identify subset relationships
- compute sums, differences, products, and quotients
- compute fractional parts of a whole

Mathematical connections

In these problems and tasks, connections are made to these other topic areas:

- arithmetic
- algebra
- geometry
- graphs
- measurement
- number theory

Problem solving strategies

Patterns and Reasoning problems and tasks offer students opportunities to use one or more of several problem solving strategies.

- **Formulate Questions:** When data are presented in displays or text form, students must pose one or more questions that can be answered using the given data.
- **Complete Stories:** When confronted with an incomplete story, students must supply the missing information and then check that the story makes sense.
- **Organize Information:** To ensure that several solution candidates for a problem are considered, students may have to organize information by drawing a picture, making a list, or constructing a table or model.
- **Guess, Check, and Revise:** In some problems, students have to identify or generate candidates for the solution and then check whether those candidates match the conditions of the problem. If the conditions are not satisfied, other possible solutions must be generated and verified.
- **Identify, Continue, and Create Patterns:** To identify the next term or terms in a sequence or to generate patterns, students have to recognize the relationship between successive terms and then generalize that relationship.
- **Use Logic:** Students have to reason deductively, from clues, to make inferences about the solution to a problem. They must reason proportionately to make trades and compute equivalent ratios. They have to reason inductively to continue patterns. They must reason spatially to mentally rotate objects.
- **Work Backward:** In some problems, the output is given and students must determine the input by identifying mathematical relationships between the input and output and applying inverse operations.

Communication skills

Problems and tasks in *Patterns and Reasoning* are designed to stimulate communication. As part of the solution process, students may have to

- describe their thinking steps
- describe patterns and rules
- find alternate solution methods and solution paths
- identify other possible answers
- formulate problems for classmates to solve
- compare estimates, solutions, and methods with classmates
- make drawings to clarify mathematical relationships

These communication skills are enhanced when students interact with one another and with the teacher. By communicating both orally and in writing, students develop their understanding and use of the language of mathematics.

How Can *Hot Math Topics* Be Used?

The problems may be used as practice of newly learned concepts and skills, as maintenance of previously learned ideas, and as enrichment experiences for early finishers or more advanced students.

They may be used in class or assigned for homework. If used during class, they may be selected to complement lessons dealing with a specific topic or assigned every week as a means of keeping skills alive and well.

Because the problems often require the application of various problem solving strategies and reasoning methods, they may also form the basis of whole-class lessons whose goals are to develop expertise with specific problem solving strategies or methods.

The problems, which are sequenced from least to most difficult, may be used by students working in pairs or on their own. The selection of problems may be made by the teacher or the students based on their needs or interests. If the plan is for students to choose problems, you may wish to copy individual problems onto card stock and laminate them, and establish a problem card file.

To facilitate record keeping, a Management Chart is provided on page 6. The chart can be duplicated so that there is one for each student. As a problem is completed, the space corresponding to that problem's number may be shaded. An Award Certificate is included on page 6 as well.

How Can Student Performance Be Assessed?

Patterns and Reasoning problems and tasks provide you with opportunities to assess students'

- pattern recognition and generation abilities
- mathematical reasoning methods
- computation ability
- problem solving abilities
- communication skills

Observations

Keeping anecdotal records helps you to remember important information you gain as you observe students at work. To make observations more manageable, limit each observation to a group of from four to six students or to one of the areas noted above. You may find that using index cards facilitates the recording process.

Discussions

Many of the *Patterns and Reasoning* problems and tasks allow for multiple answers or may be solved in a variety of ways. This built-in richness motivates students to discuss their work with one another. Small groups or class discussions are appropriate. As students share their approaches to the problems, you will gain additional insights into their content knowledge, mathematical reasoning, and communication abilities.

Scoring responses

You may wish to holistically score students' responses to the problems and tasks. The simple scoring rubric below uses three levels: high, medium, and low.

High	Medium	Low
• Solution demonstrates that the student knows the concepts and skills. • Solution is complete and thorough. • The student communicates effectively.	• Solution demonstrates that the student has some knowledge of the concepts and skills. • Solution is complete. • The student communicates somewhat clearly.	• Solution shows that the student has little or no grasp of the concepts and skills. • Solution is incomplete or contains major errors. • The student does not communicate effectively.

Portfolios

Having students store their responses to the problems in *Hot Math Topics* portfolios allows them to see improvement in their work over time. You may want to have them choose examples of their best responses for inclusion in their permanent portfolios, accompanied by explanations as to why each was chosen.

Students and the assessment process

Involving students in the assessment process is central to the development of their abilities to reflect on their own work, to understand the assessment standards to which they are held accountable, and to take ownership for their own learning. Young children may find the reflective process difficult, but with your coaching, they can develop such skills.

Discussion may be needed to help students better understand your standards for performance. Ask students such questions as, "What does it mean to communicate *clearly*?" "What is a *complete* response?" Some students may want to use a rubric to score their responses.

Participation in peer-assessment tasks will also help students to better understand the performance standards. In pairs or small groups, students can review each other's responses and offer feedback. Opportunities to revise work may then be given.

What Additional Materials Are Needed?

Crayons, a book, color chips, paper clips, rulers, straws, scissors, and square tiles in red, blue, green, and yellow are required for solving the problems in *Patterns and Reasoning*. Other manipulatives and materials may be helpful, including hundreds charts; toothpicks; models of a cylinder, cube, sphere, and rectangular prism; play money; and an almanac.

Management Chart Name ______________________

When a problem or task is completed, shade the box with that number.

1	2	3	4	5	6	7	8	9	10
11	12	13	14	15	16	17	18	19	20
21	22	23	24	25	26	27	28	29	30
31	32	33	34	35	36	37	38	39	40
41	42	43	44	45	46	47	48	49	50
51	52	53	54	55	56	57	58	59	60
61	62	63	64	65	66	67	68	69	70
71	72	73	74	75	76	77	78	79	80
81	82	83	84	85	86	87	88	89	90
91	92	93	94	95	96	97	98	99	100

Award Certificate

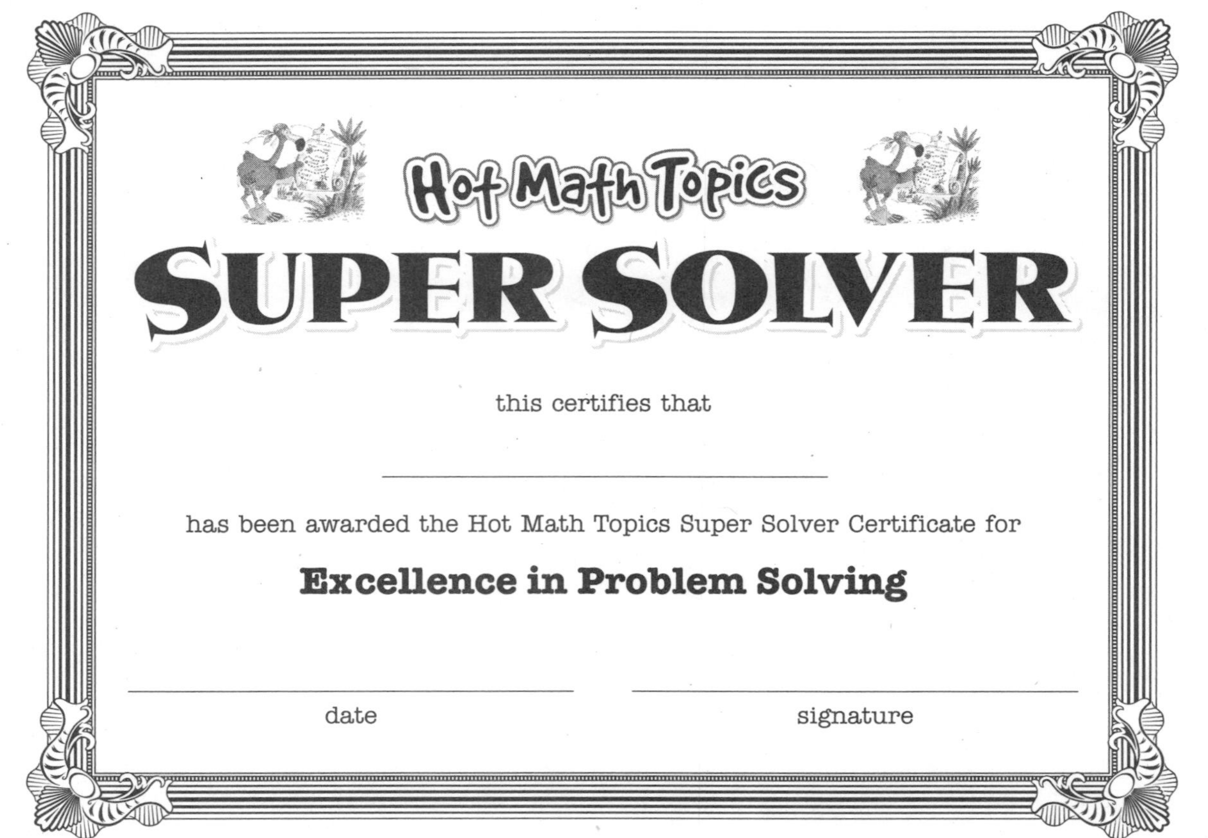

©Addison Wesley Longman, Inc./Published by Dale Seymour Publications®

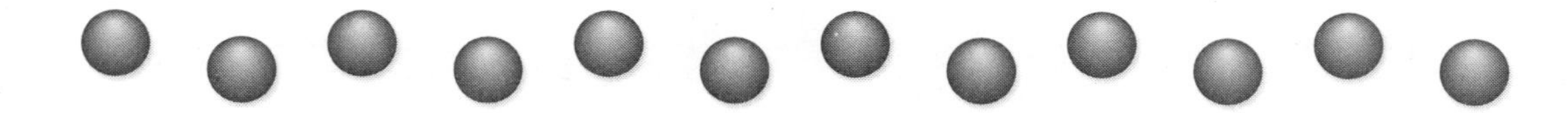

Problems and Tasks

1

- Ken is older than Danya.
- Maria is in high school.
- Brett is 2 years younger than Ken.

Ken is ______ years old. **Maria is ______ years old.**

Danya is ______ years old. **Brett is ______ years old.**

2

Which shape does not belong?

Why?

A B C D

Choose a different shape.

Tell why it doesn't belong.

©Addison Wesley Longman, Inc./Published by Dale Seymour Publications®

Fill in the circles.

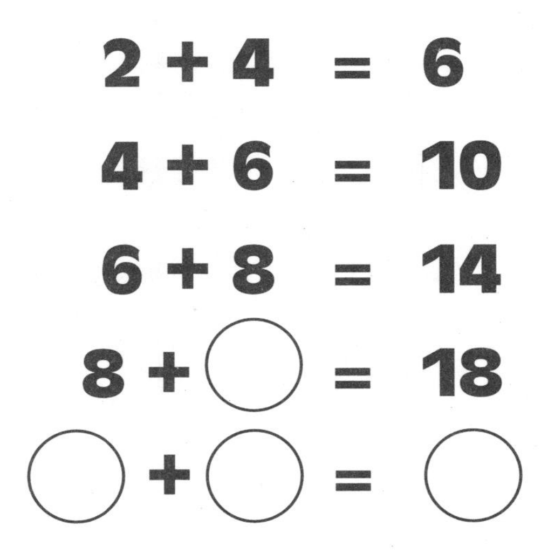

Tell about the patterns you see.

Bus Schedule			
Leave		**Arrive**	
Mathopolis	9:15	Logictown	11:30
		Reasonville	12:05
		Pattern Corner	1:45
		Think City	2:00
Mathopolis	11:00	Logictown	1:05
		Reasonville	1:45
		Pattern Corner	3:15
		Think City	4:15

Where did Kiara get off the bus?

- She left Mathopolis at 9:15.
- She rode the bus for more than 4 hours.
- She did not go to Think City.

These tiles are not in order.

How would you order them to make a pattern?

Describe your pattern.

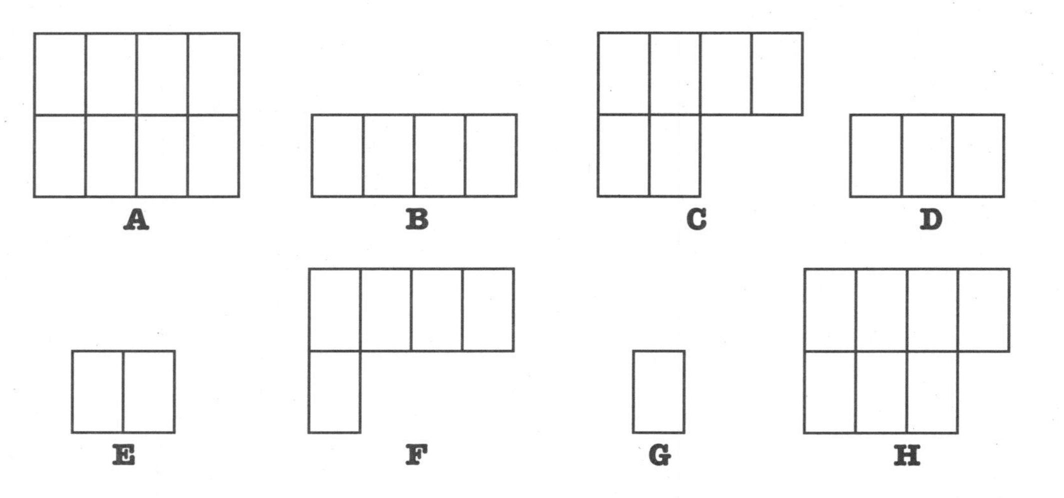

Order them a different way. Describe the new pattern.

6

Get a partner.

Take turns.

One person picks a number from 1 to 100.

To guess the number, the other person asks questions that can be answered yes or no.

7

This is a pattern of letters.

The pattern continues for 32 letters.

How many A's are in the pattern?

Tell how you know.

8

Use the facts.

Write the name under each boy.

Facts

- Taylor is directly in front of Kiran.
- Carl is directly in front of Mac.
- José is in the middle.
- Mac is not last.

©Addison Wesley Longman, Inc./Published by Dale Seymour Publications®

Which number does not belong?

Tell how you decided.

1 6 7 27

Is another answer possible?

I got on the elevator.

I rode up 2 floors.

I rode down 3 floors.

I got out on floor 7.

On what floor did I get into the elevator?

Blake, Amos, and Larson each play an instrument.

One plays the flute, one plays the piano, and one plays the guitar.

- Blake does not play the guitar.
- Amos does not play the flute.
- Larson does not play the flute or the guitar.

Tell who plays which instrument.

©Addison Wesley Longman, Inc./Published by Dale Seymour Publications®

Count by 3s.
Color each number yellow.

Count by 6s.
Color each number blue.

Write about the patterns you see.

Talk with a friend about your patterns.

1	2	3	4	5	6	7	8	9	10
11	12	13	14	15	16	17	18	19	20
21	22	23	24	25	26	27	28	29	30
31	32	33	34	35	36	37	38	39	40
41	42	43	44	45	46	47	48	49	50
51	52	53	54	55	56	57	58	59	60
61	62	63	64	65	66	67	68	69	70
71	72	73	74	75	76	77	78	79	80
81	82	83	84	85	86	87	88	89	90
91	92	93	94	95	96	97	98	99	100

Imagine that you cut a square in half.

Then, imagine that you cut the halves in half.

You do this two more times.

How many pieces would you have?

Make a pattern using circles, squares, and triangles.

Draw the pattern.

Have a friend decide what comes next.

The clocks show important times in Myra's classroom on Tuesday.

They show the times for gym, library, math, and art.

- Library time is 45 minutes before art time.
- Math starts 40 minutes after gym class.

Write the times in order and tell what happens.

Time	What Happens

Draw the missing tile design.

Tell how you decided what to draw.

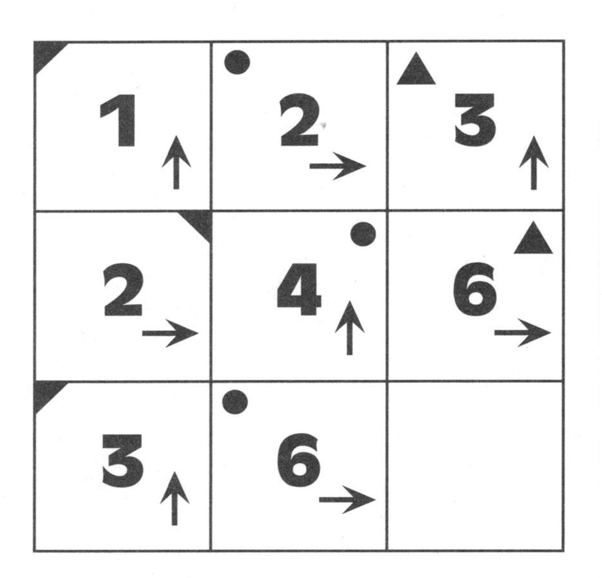

The scale is balanced.

Which is heavier, weight A or weight B?

How do you know?

A A B

What else do you know about the weights?

19

Two containers can hold the same amount of liquid.

Do they have to be the same shape?

Explain your thinking.

Use drawings in your explanation.

20

Write a number on each jersey.

Be sure the numbers fit the facts.

Facts

- Pedro's number is odd.
- Tanya's number is even.
- Margo's number is the greatest number.
- Kiki's number is twice Pedro's number.

Use each number in the table for the start number.

Find the end number.

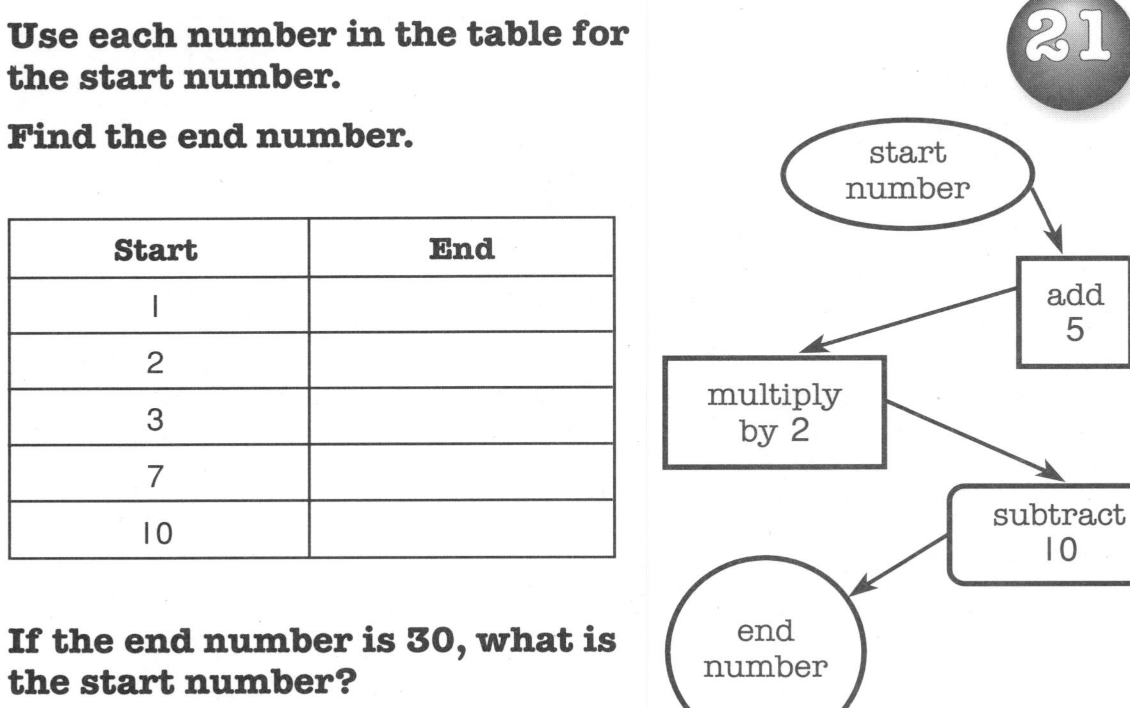

Start	End
1	
2	
3	
7	
10	

If the end number is 30, what is the start number?

Write chain 5 and chain 6.

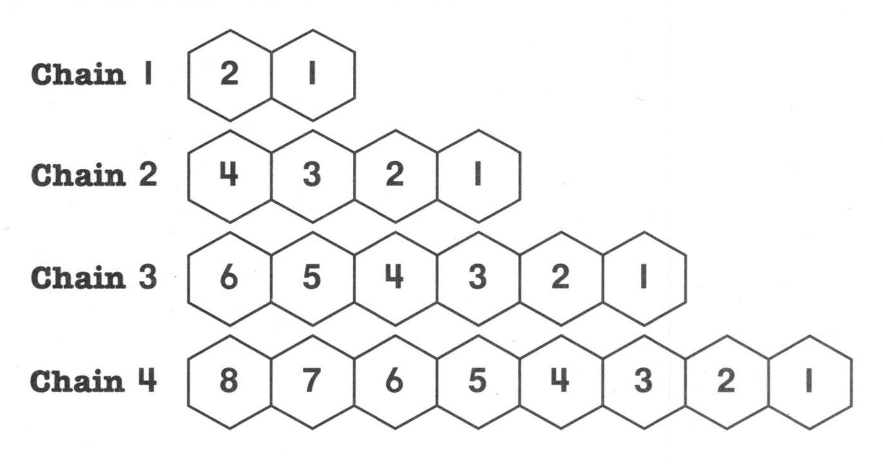

Chain 5

Chain 6

What is the first number in chain 10?

What is the second number in chain 40?

Look for patterns.

23

Set 1

Set 2

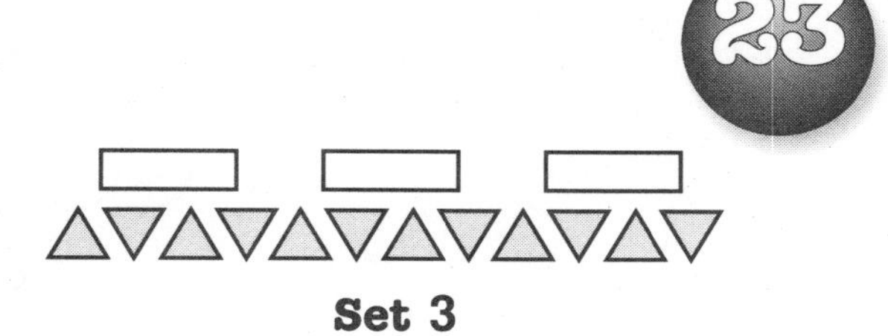

Set 3

Think about set 10.

How many rectangles?

How many triangles?

Think about set 30.

How many rectangles?

How many triangles?

Who is who?

Write the correct name on each shirt.

Katie says,
"I have an even number.
You don't say my number
when you count by 4s."

Ellen says,
"My number is odd!
You can only divide
it by 1 and by itself."

Daryl says,
"When you divide my number
by 7, the quotient is the same
as the ones digit."

Vic says,
"My number is special!
If you multiply some number
by itself, you get my number."

©Addison Wesley Longman, Inc./Published by Dale Seymour Publications®

25

Open a book.

Add the numbers on the facing pages.

Is the sum odd or even?

Do it again. Is the sum odd or even?

Will this always be true? Why?

I am an odd number.

If you add me to myself, the total is between 30 and 35.

What number am I?

I am an even number.

If you add 10 to me, the total is between 16 and 20.

What number am I?

I am an odd number.

If you subtract 2 from me, the difference is between 1 and 5.

What number am I?

©Addison Wesley Longman, Inc./Published by Dale Seymour Publications®

326 24 36 18

27

Complete these sentences about the numbers above.

All of these numbers are . . .

None of these numbers are . . .

Some of these numbers are . . .

Compare your sentences with a friend's sentences.

28

The pattern continues.

Draw building 5.

Tell the number of △ and □.

building 1 — 1△ 3□

building 2 — 2△ 6□

building 3 — 3△ 9□

building 4 — 4△ 12□

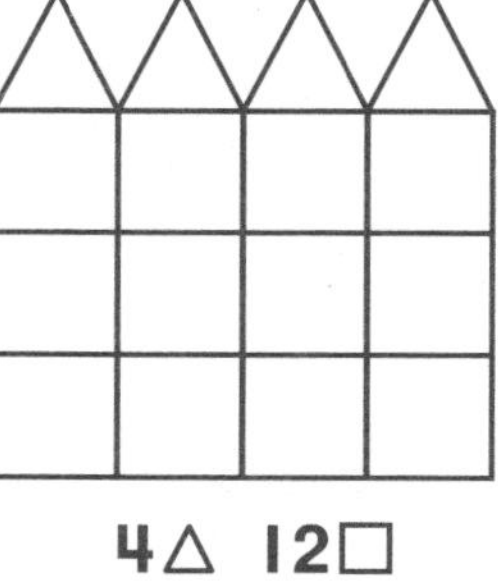

How many △ are in building 20?

How many □ are in building 20?

©Addison Wesley Longman, Inc./Published by Dale Seymour Publications®

The pattern continues.

What is the 34th letter?

Tell how you know.

The pattern continues.

What is the 41st shape?

Tell how you know.

What numbers do A, B, and C stand for?

Find other solutions.

What is always true about C? Why?

What is always true about B? Why?

©Addison Wesley Longman, Inc./Published by Dale Seymour Publications®

How many pages are there in my book?

- There are between 100 and 800 pages.
- Each digit is the same.
- The sum of the digits is 12.

In what row is 21 the second number?
Tell how you know.

What is the third number in row 10?
Tell how you know.

In what row is the sum 45?
Tell how you know.

Row 1 $1 + 2 + 3 = 6$

Row 2 $2 + 3 + 4 = 9$

Row 3 $3 + 4 + 5 = 12$

Row 4 $4 + 5 + 6 = 15$

Row 5

Row 6

Write two more questions about the pattern.
Trade questions with a classmate.

Maggie is standing in line.

How many people are in line?

How do you know?

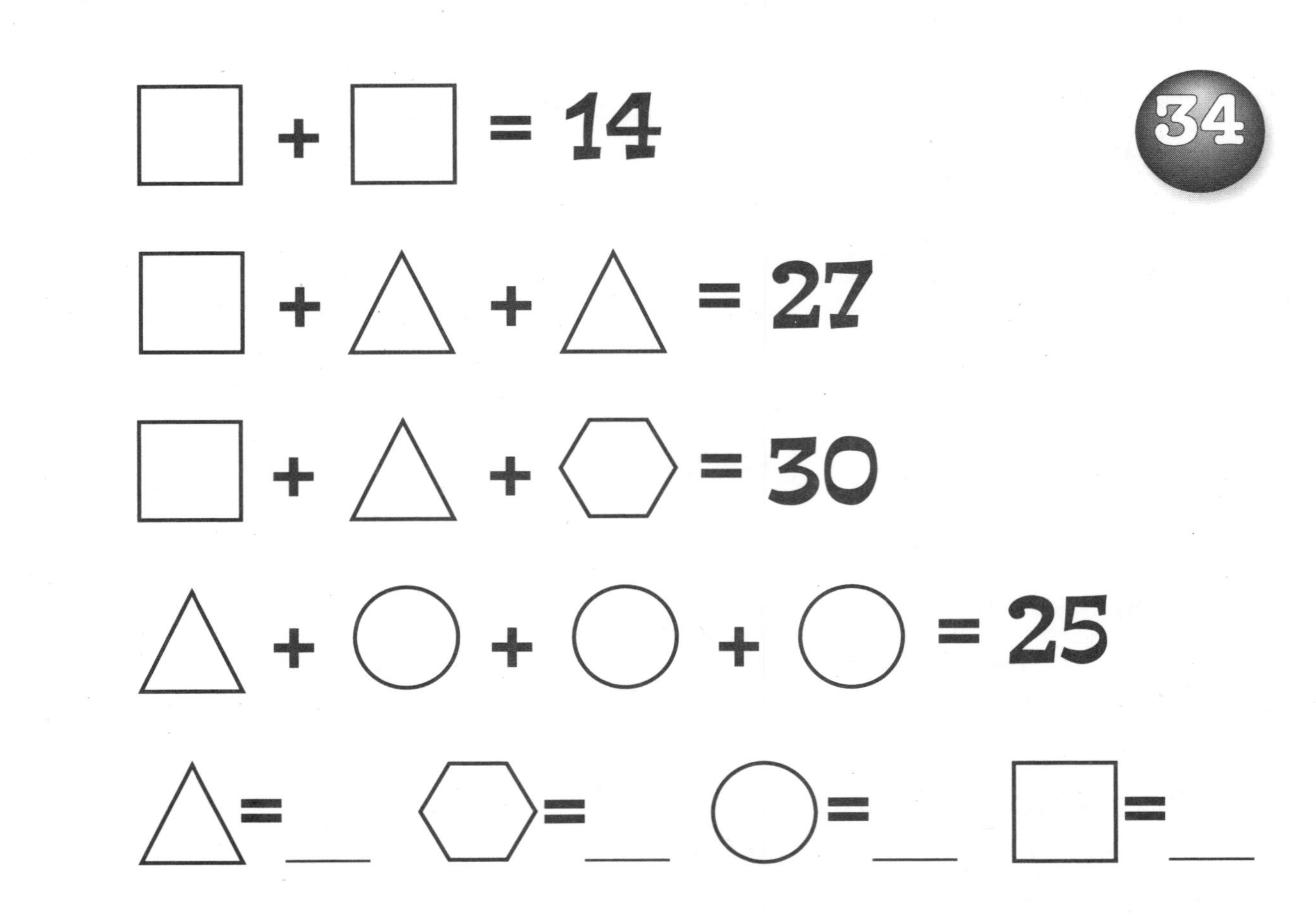

35

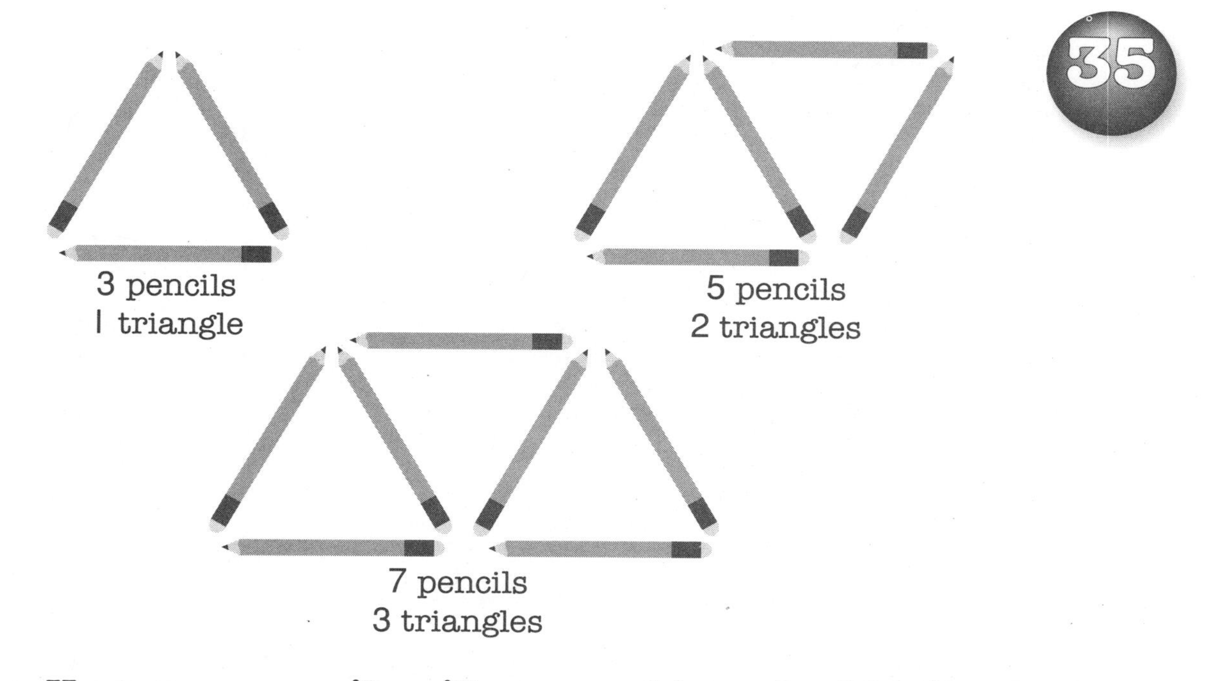

How many pencils will you need to make 10 triangles?

How do you know?

The pattern continues.

Fill in the blanks.

$$3 \times 5 + 1 = 4 \times 4$$

$$5 \times 7 + 1 = 6 \times 6$$

$$7 \times 9 + 1 = \_\_\_ \times \_\_\_$$

$$9 \times \_\_\_ + 1 = \_\_\_ \times \_\_\_$$

Describe 3 patterns you see.

©Addison Wesley Longman, Inc./Published by Dale Seymour Publications®

37

Use the clues.

Find the number of the gift.

Clues

- The number is less than 13 + 7.
- The number is greater than 3 × 4.
- The number is not even.

The number is _____.

Pick another number from the gifts.

Write clues.

Have a friend find your number.

38

MYSTERY NUMBERS

- Mystery Numbers have 3 digits.
- The sum of the digits in a Mystery Number is 10.
- In a Mystery Number, the hundreds digit is the same as the tens digit.

List the Mystery Numbers.

Check with a friend to make sure you have found all the possibilities.

39

Who is who?

- Leah doesn't have any brothers.
- Alan and Bakari have the same number of brothers.
- Monika is younger than Alan.

***W* is ________________.**

***X* is ________________.**

***Y* is ________________.**

***Z* is ________________.**

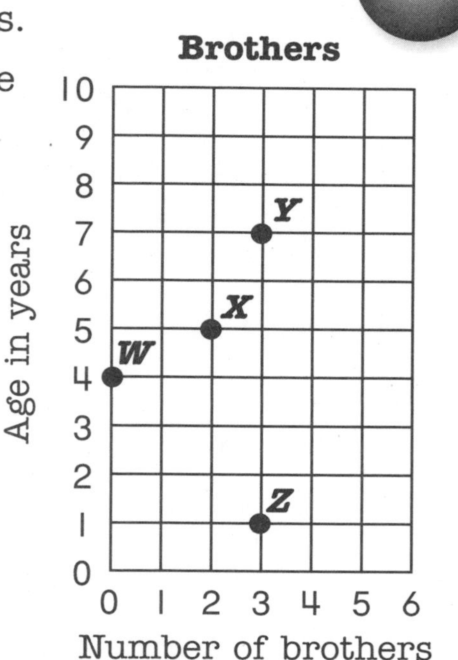

40

Use the numbers next to the map.

Fill in the blanks.

The state with the greatest number of people is California. It has ________ people.

The largest city in the state is Los Angeles. It has ________ people.

San Diego, with between 1 and 2 million people, or ________ people, is the second largest city in California.

There are ________ more people in Los Angeles than in San Diego.

©Addison Wesley Longman, Inc./Published by Dale Seymour Publications®

There are 60 jelly beans in the pattern.

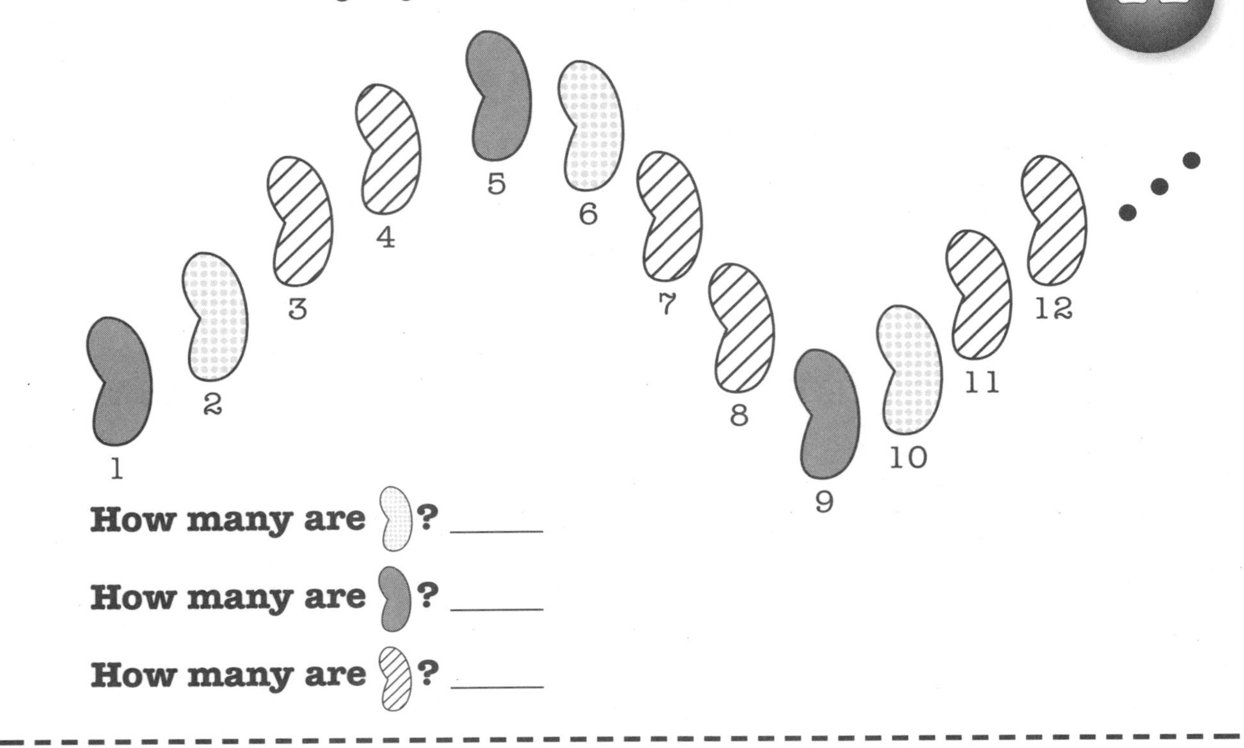

How many are (dotted)**?** _____

How many are (dark)**?** _____

How many are (striped)**?** _____

Use the facts.

Write each child's name.

Pick an age for each child that fits the facts.

Facts

- Alex is older than Stacy.
- Stacy is younger than Pat.
- Pat is younger than Alex.

Facts

- Ruben is twice as old as Pia.
- The sum of their ages is 27.

Rueben is _____ years old.

Pia is _____ years old.

The number pattern continues.

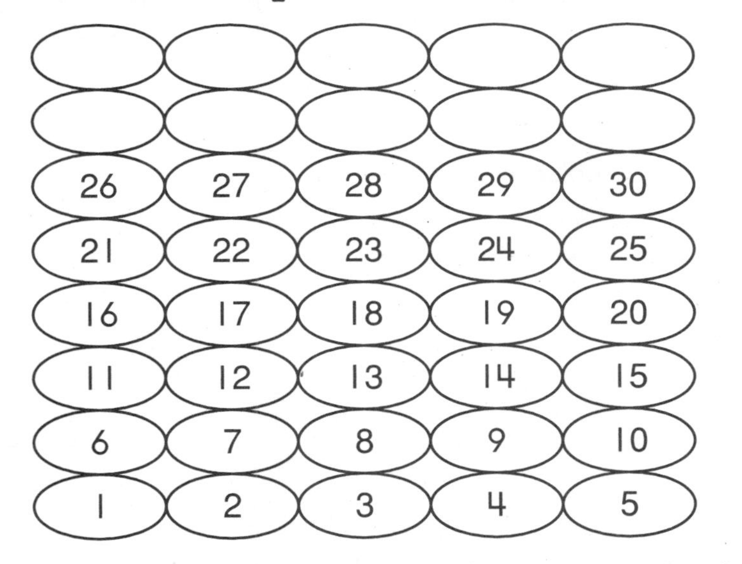

Follow the arrows to fill in the missing numbers.

3 ↑ = 8	**8 ↓ = 3**	**16 ↑ = 21**	**21 ↓↓ = 11**
2 ↑ = _____	**14 ↑ = _____**	**25 ↓ = _____**	**16 ↓ = _____**
23 ↑↑ = _____	**25 ↓↓ = _____**	**27 ↑↑↑ = _____**	**35 ↓↓↑ = _____**

©Addison Wesley Longman, Inc./Published by Dale Seymour Publications®

45

Matthew, Molly, and Paul are each on a different school team.

One is on the swim team, one is on the golf team, and one is on the tennis team.

Molly's sport does not use a ball.

Matthew has never played a game on a court.

Who is on which team?

46

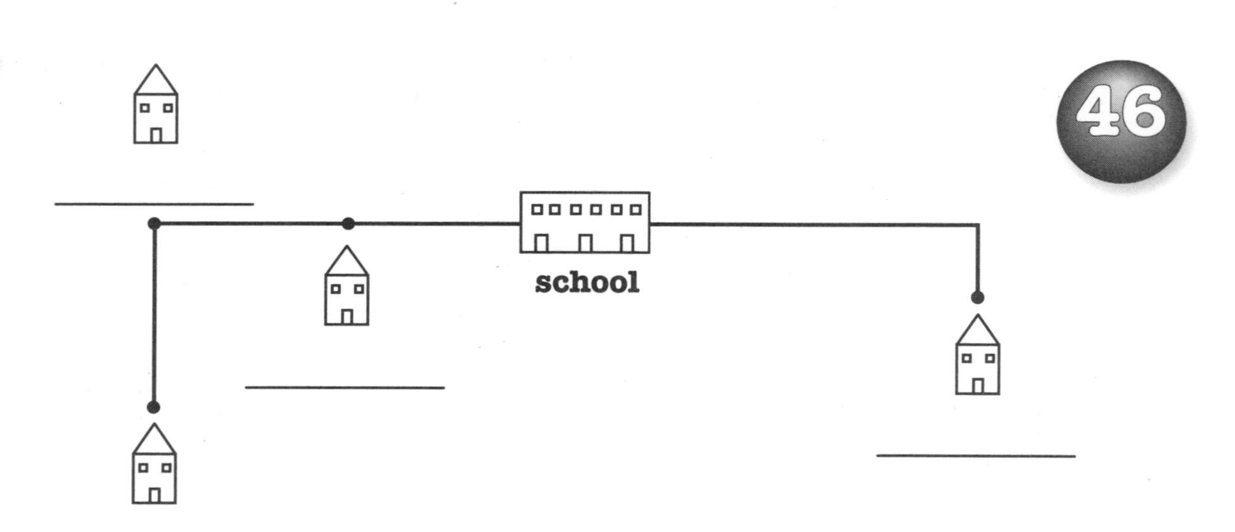

Write the names of the students under the houses.

- Tami lives farthest from school.
- Alex lives closer to school than Hani does.
- Nathan lives the closest to school.

My grandmother visits me tomorrow.

The day before yesterday was Tuesday.

On what day is my grandmother visiting?

I saw a play last month.

Tomorrow we celebrate New Year's Day.

In what month did I see a play?

Work with a partner.

Complete the sentences about these shapes.

All of these shapes are ______________________________ .

Some of these shapes are ______________________________ .

None of these shapes are ______________________________ .

Which is heavier, 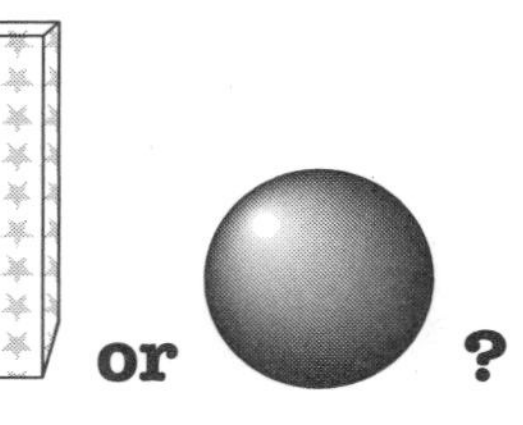 or ?

How can you tell?

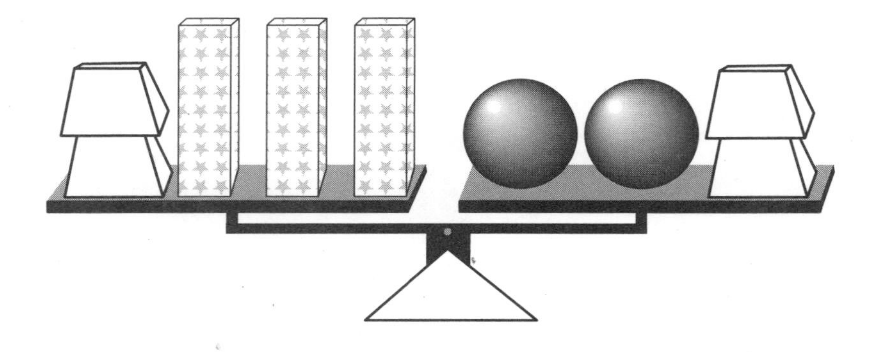

50

Aleta, Brigitte, and Terry have their birthdays on the same day.

- Aleta's age added to Brigitte's age is 16 years.
- Aleta is older than Brigitte.
- Terry is younger than Aleta and older than Brigitte.

If Terry was 13 years old on her birthday, how old could Brigitte be?

Explain your thinking.

HAPPY BIRTHDAY

51

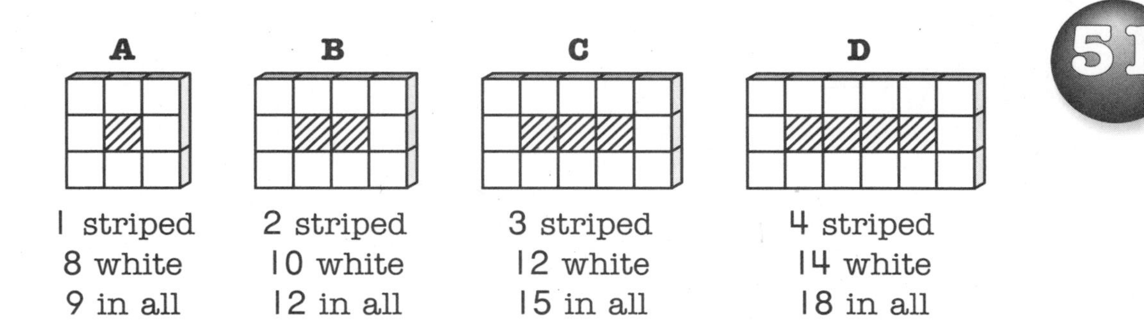

Imagine figure E.

- How many cubes will be striped?
- How many cubes will be white?
- How many cubes will there be in all?

How do you know?

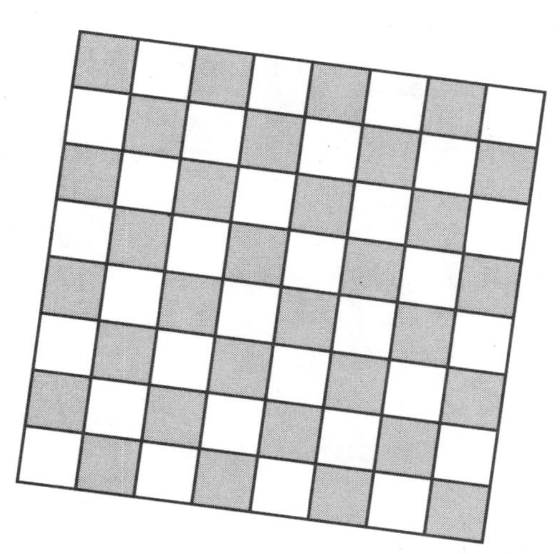

Louisa, Tracy, Chantel, Tia, and Opal are playing checkers.

Each girl plays one game with each of the other girls.

How many games of checkers do they play?

Tell how you know.

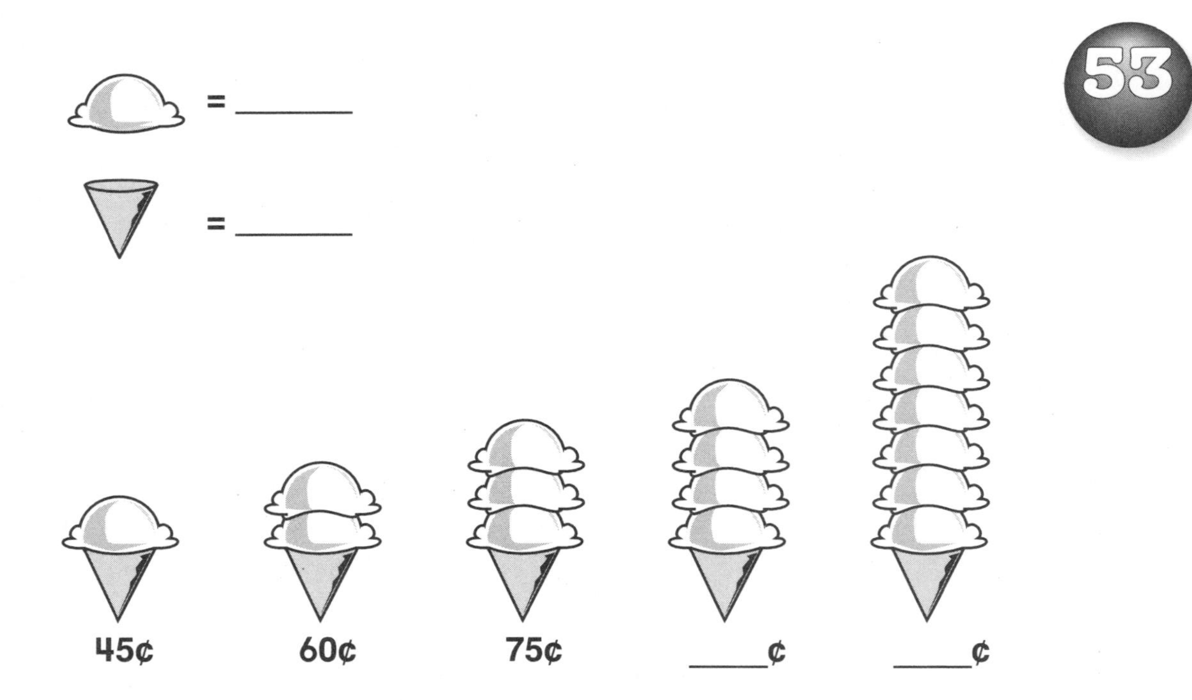

54

2590 2541 2399 2449 2400

Use the clues to find the number.

Clues

- It is less than 2590.
- It is more than 2399.
- There is a 4 in the tens place.
- The hundreds digit is greater than the ones digit.

What is the number?

©Addison Wesley Longman, Inc./Published by Dale Seymour Publications®

55

The walls are made of cubes.

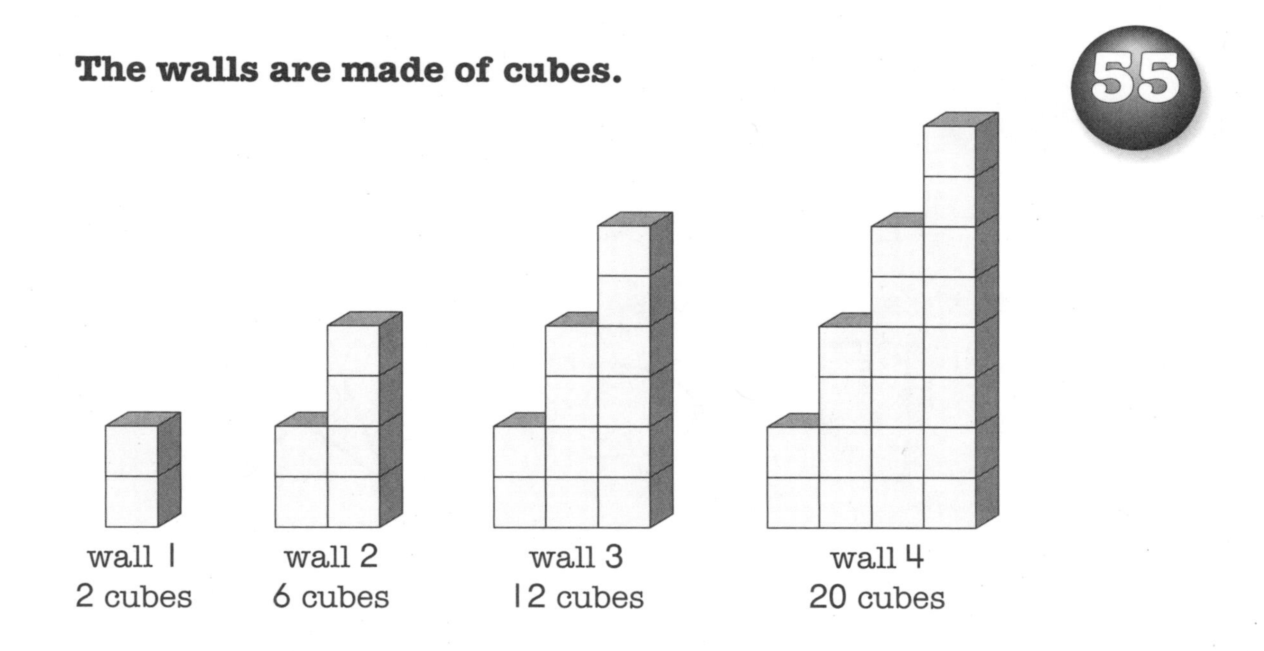

How many cubes are in wall 6?

Tell how you know.

56

Jack ate half of a pizza.

Halle ate one piece of pizza.

Halle ate more pizza than Jack.

How is this possible?

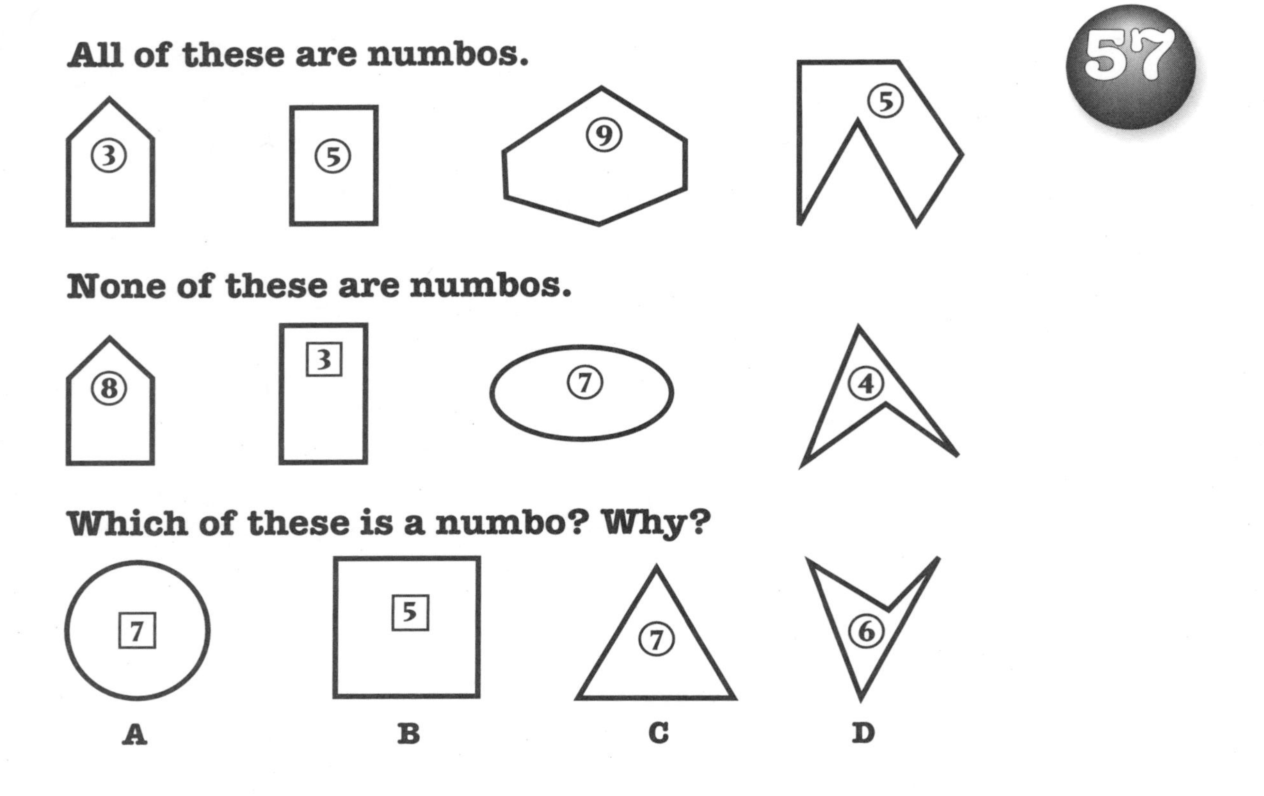

MAGICAL MATH

58

Start with any number. _____

Add 20. _____

Subtract 17. _____

Subtract 3. _____

Multiply by 2. _____

Divide by 2. _____

What do you notice about your answer?

Try a different starting number.

Why do you think this happens?

In which row and column will you find 37?

Tell how you know.

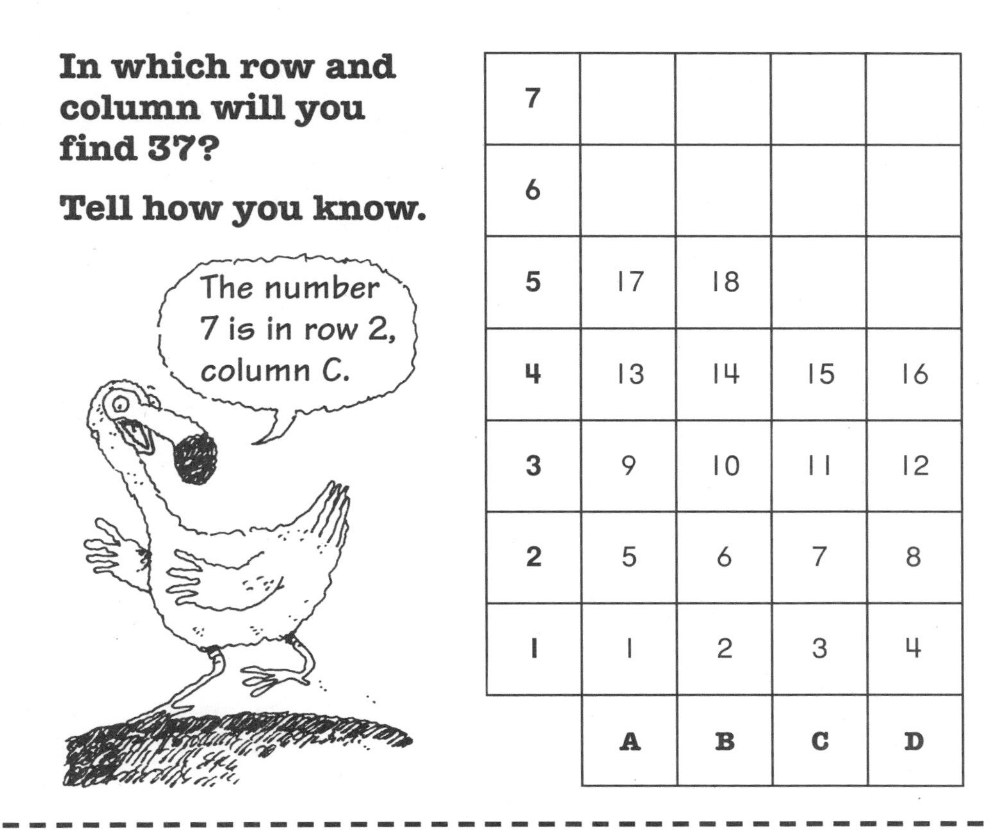

7				
6				
5	17	18		
4	13	14	15	16
3	9	10	11	12
2	5	6	7	8
1	1	2	3	4
	A	**B**	**C**	**D**

Use the facts.

Write the last names of the presidents on the lines.

President's Birthdays

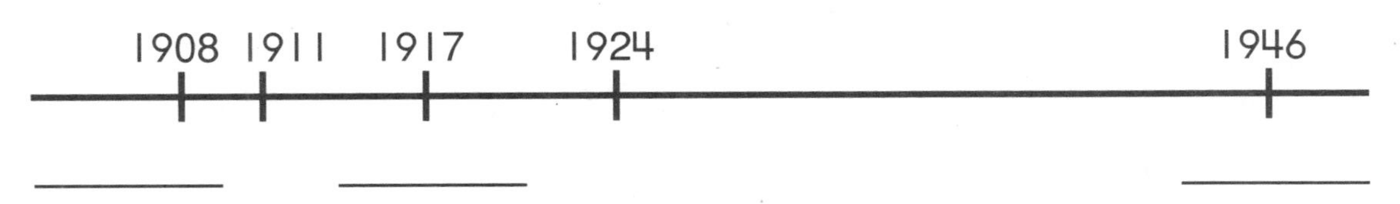

Facts

George Bush	Born when Johnson was almost 16.
William Clinton	Kennedy was 29 when Clinton was born.
John Kennedy	Born after Reagan but before Bush.
Ronald Reagan	Born after Johnson.
Lyndon Johnson	Born 38 years before Clinton.

©Addison Wesley Longman, Inc./Published by Dale Seymour Publications®

61

Isabelle counted by 2s from 2 to 100.

Monica counted by 4s from 4 to 100.

Celine counted by 5s from 5 to 100.

What same numbers did they all say?

Play this game with a partner.

Get 4 blue, 4 red, 4 green, and 4 yellow tiles.

Use a 4-by-4 grid.

Make a pattern on the grid.

Directions

- Take turns.
- Player 1 closes his or her eyes.
- Player 2 takes away 1 tile of each color and keeps a record of where the different colors belong.
- Player 1 guesses where each color tile belongs.

©Addison Wesley Longman, Inc./Published by Dale Seymour Publications®

What's the number?

Use the clues.

Clues

- You say the number when you count by 2s, by 3s, and by 5s.
- The number is between 50 and 100.
- The number is not divisible by 4.

These squares are made with toothpicks.

The pattern continues.

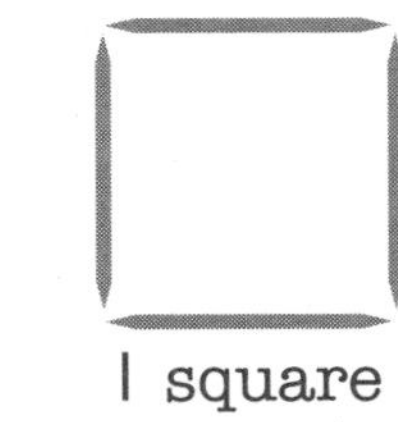

1 square	2 squares	3 squares
4 toothpicks	7 toothpicks	10 toothpicks

How many toothpicks do you need to make 6 squares?

To make 10 squares?

To make 100 squares?

Tell how you know.

©Addison Wesley Longman, Inc./Published by Dale Seymour Publications®

Tanya made a string of 72 beads.

This is part of her string.

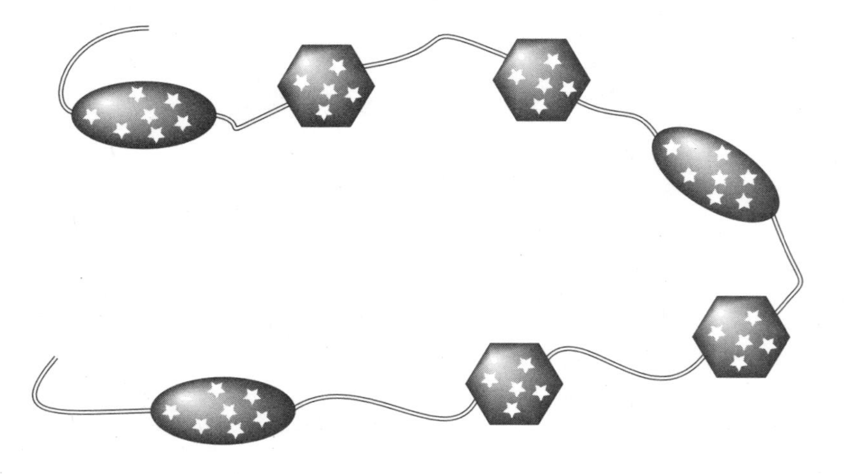

How many are in her bead string?

Tell how you know.

Describe this number pattern in two ways.

4 8 12 16 20

If the pattern continues, what number will be 26th in the line?

Tell how you know.

©Addison Wesley Longman, Inc./Published by Dale Seymour Publications®

All of these are frapples.

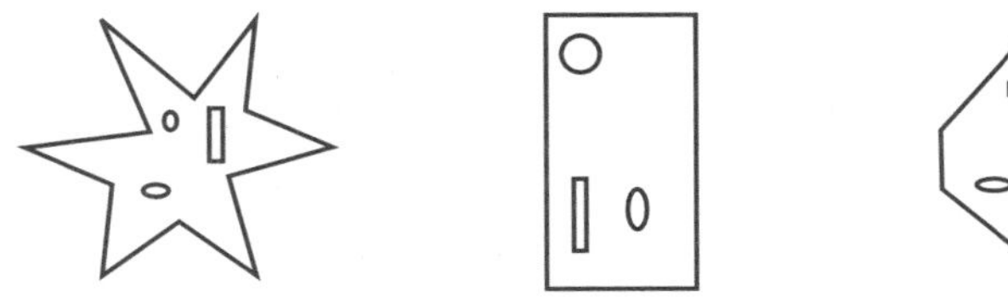
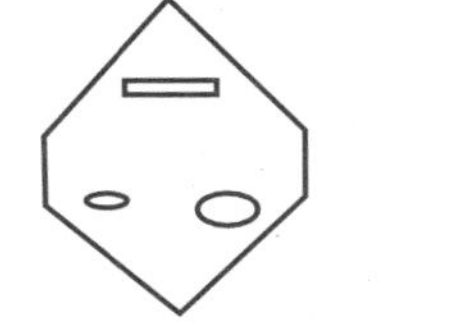
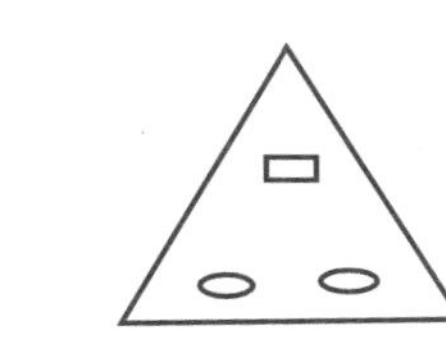

None of these are frapples.

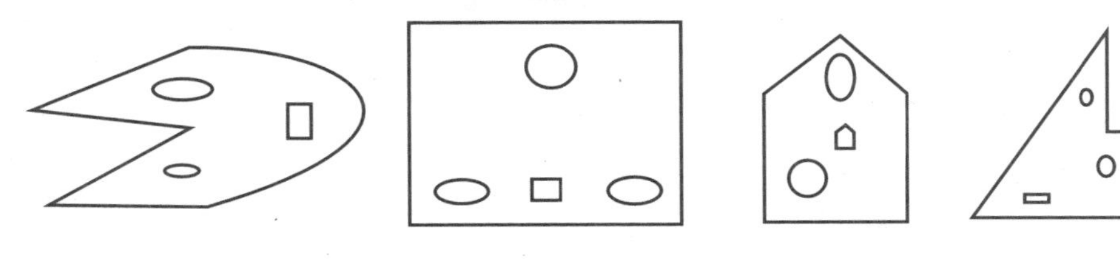

Which of these are frapples? Why?

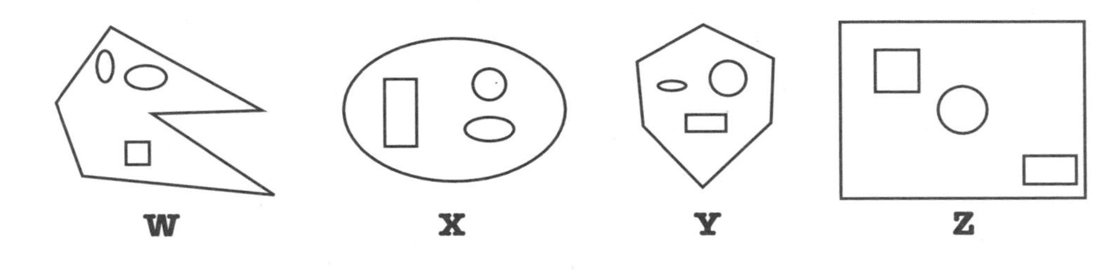

What is the number?

Use the clues.

Clues

- It is between 6 × 20 and 700 ÷ 5.
- It is even.
- Its tens digit is one more than its ones digit.

Record the steps you use to find the number.

©Addison Wesley Longman, Inc./Published by Dale Seymour Publications®

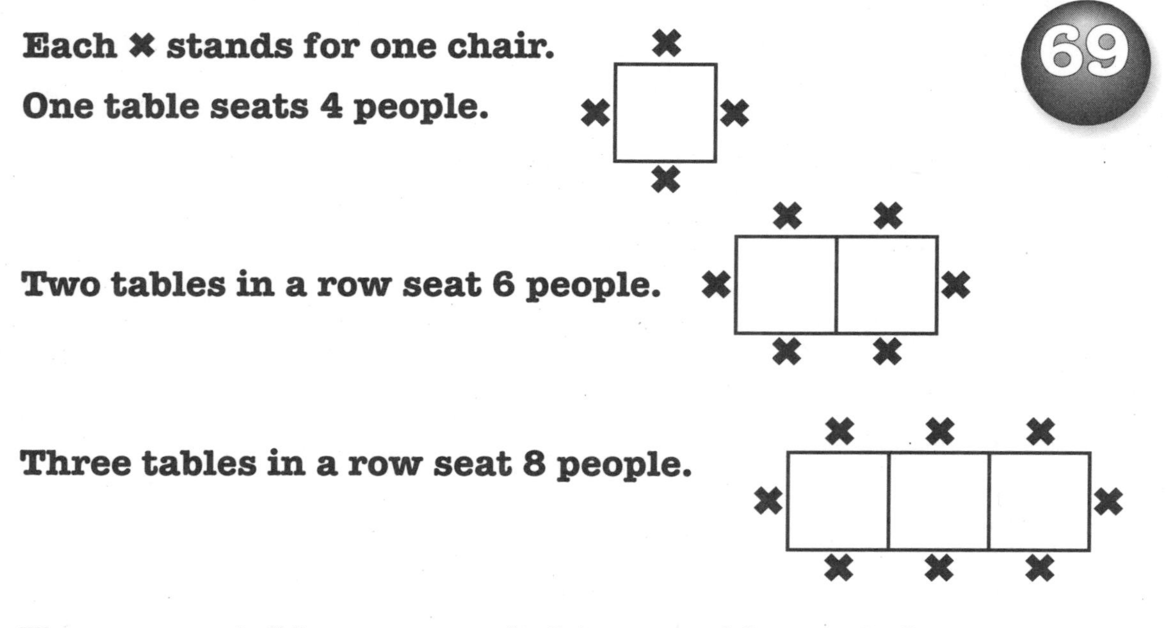

69

Each ✖ stands for one chair.

One table seats 4 people.

Two tables in a row seat 6 people.

Three tables in a row seat 8 people.

How many tables are needed to seat 48 people?

Tell how you know.

Caleb, Doug, and Edward each have a dog.

The names of their dogs are Chow, Dowser, and Eggie.

The names of the boys and their dogs do not begin with the same letter.

The names of the boys and their dogs do not have the same number of letters.

Who owns which dog?

1	2	3	4	5	6	7	8	9	10
11	12	13	14	15	16	17	18	19	20
21	22	23	24	25	26	27	28	29	30
31	32	33	34	35	36	37	38	39	40
41	42	43	44	45	46	47	48	49	50
51	52	53	54	55	56	57	58	59	60

Ring each number you say when you count by 4s.

Make an X on each number you say when you count by 8s.

What numbers between 80 and 100 will have both a ring and an X?

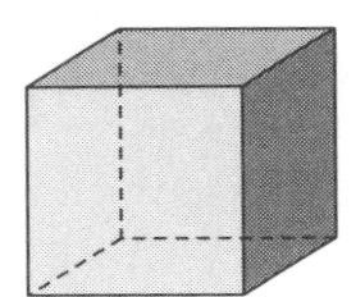
cube

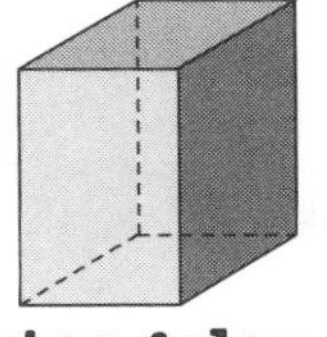
rectangular prism

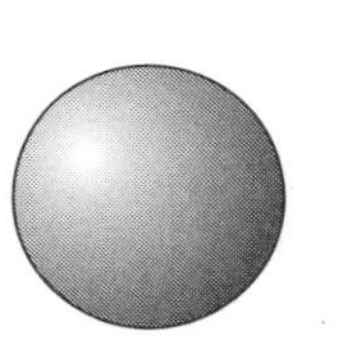
sphere

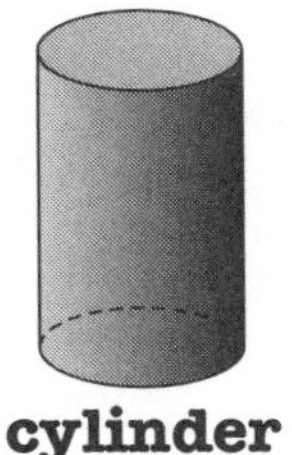
cylinder

Use the facts to find the shape.

Facts

- It slides when pushed.
- It does not have any curves.
- Its faces are not all the same size.

Choose a different shape.

Write your own facts.

Have a friend use your facts to find the shape.

©Addison Wesley Longman, Inc./Published by Dale Seymour Publications®

73

Noah first drew figure A.

He then made this pattern by turning and flipping the figure.

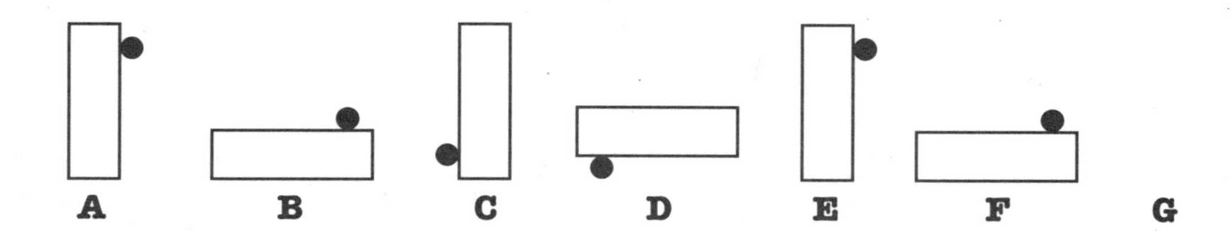

Tell how to turn and flip each figure to make the next figure.

Draw figure G in Noah's pattern.

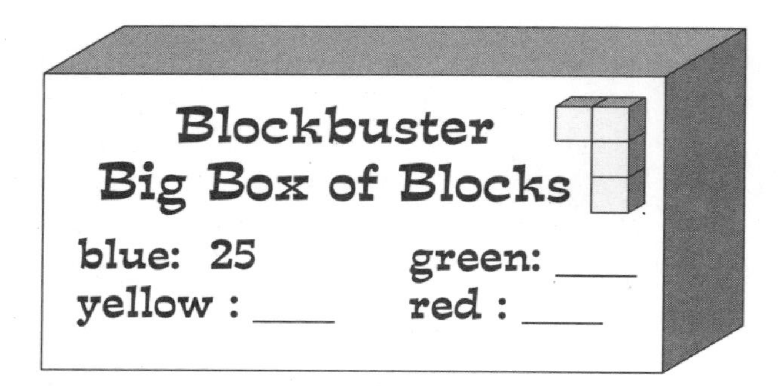

The box shows only the number of blue blocks.

Use the facts to write the number of blocks of each color.

Facts

- There are twice as many green blocks as blue blocks.
- There are the same number of red blocks as yellow blocks.
- There are 85 blocks altogether.

How many beads are in this bead chain?

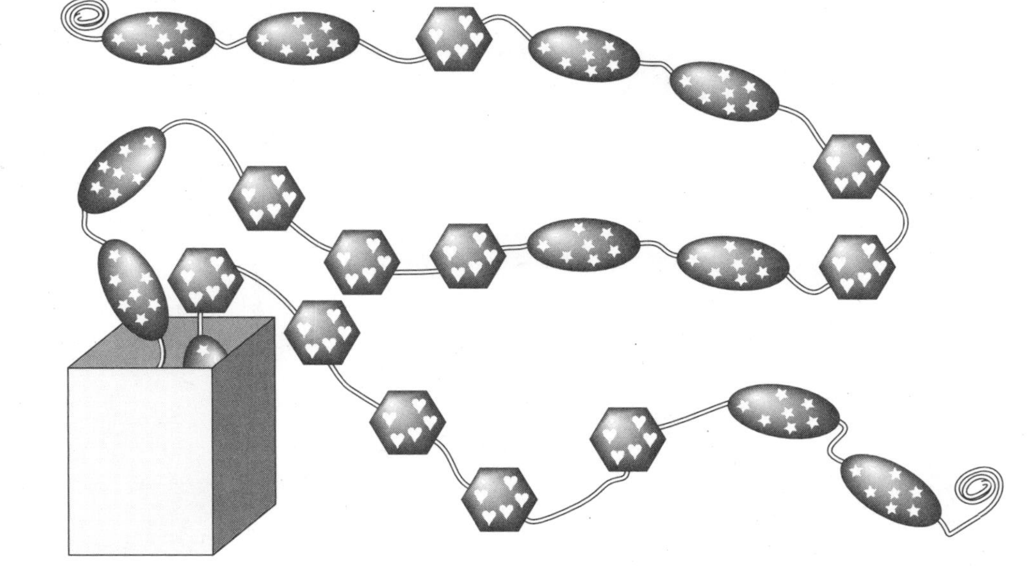

How did you find out?

76

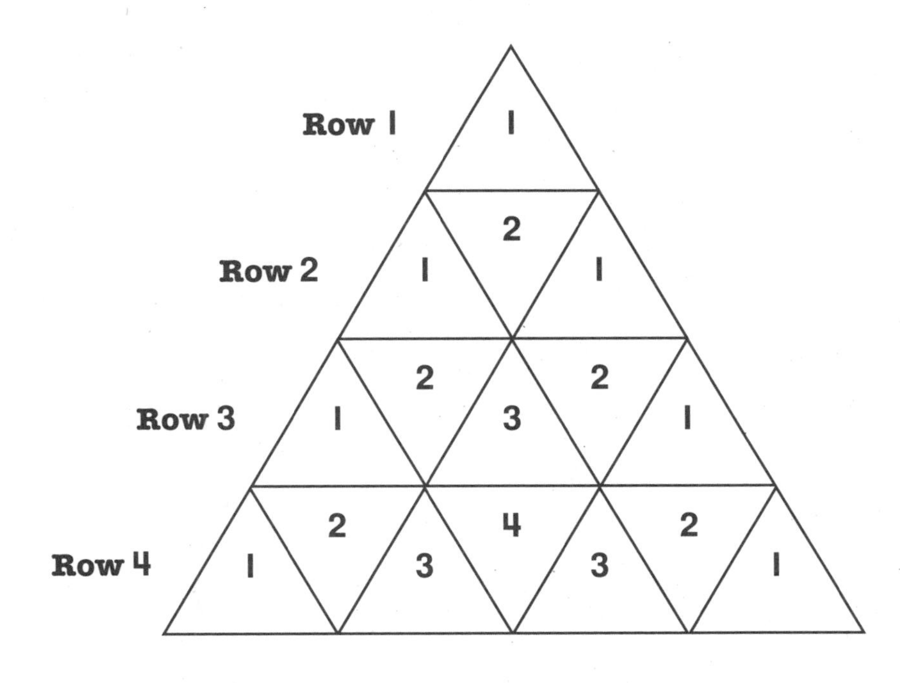

How many numbers are in row 10?

Tell how you know.

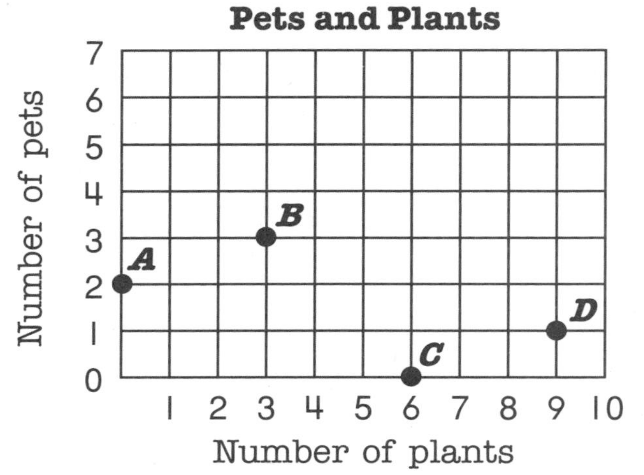

77

Who is who?

- Delia doesn't have any pets.
- Eric has 9 plants and a dog.
- Jin Lee doesn't have any plants.
- Thomas has the same number of plants as pets.

A **is** ________________ .

B **is** ________________ .

C **is** ________________ .

D **is** ________________ .

78

Danny, Ang, and Tomas walked heel-to-toe across the room.

They counted their steps.

Danny took 3 steps for every step Ang took.

Tomas took half as many steps as Danny.

Ang took 20 steps.

How many steps did Danny take?

How many steps did Tomas take?

Eva, Stef, and Gia each drew an animal.

One drew a parrot, one drew a mouse, and one drew a dog.

Use the facts to figure out who drew which animal.

Facts

- Gia's animal has 4 legs.
- Eva's animal does not bark.
- Stef did not draw a mouse.
- Eva's animal does not fly.

Eva drew the ________ .

Stef drew the ________ .

Gia drew the ________ .

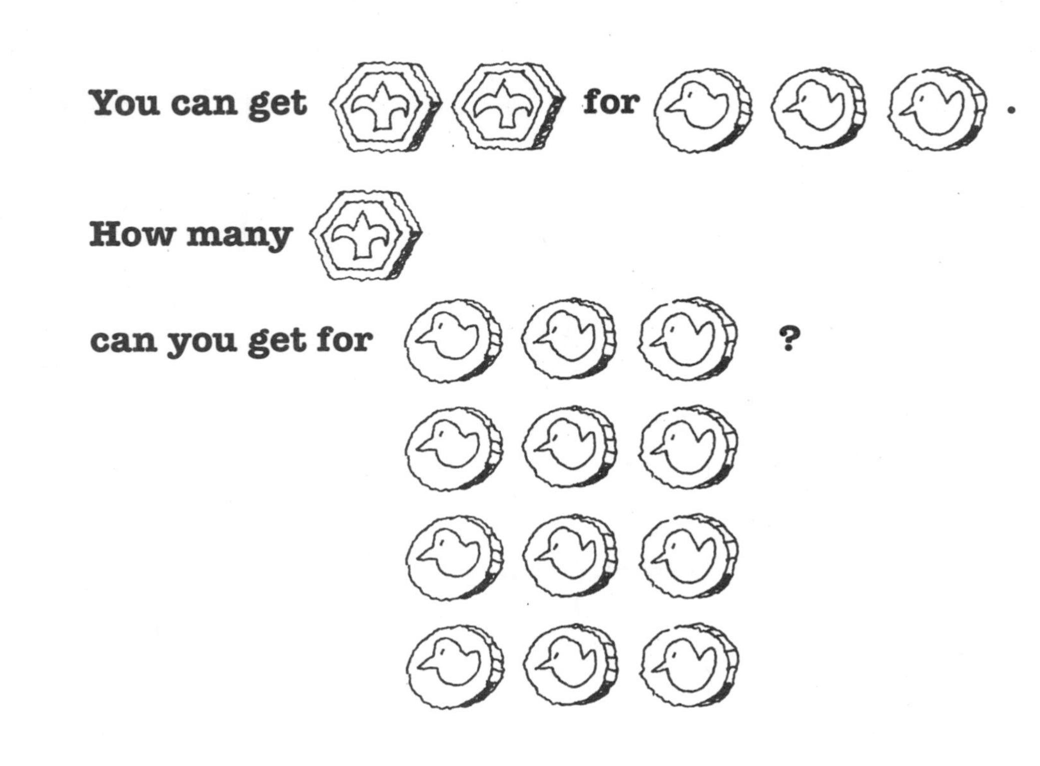

What comes next?

81

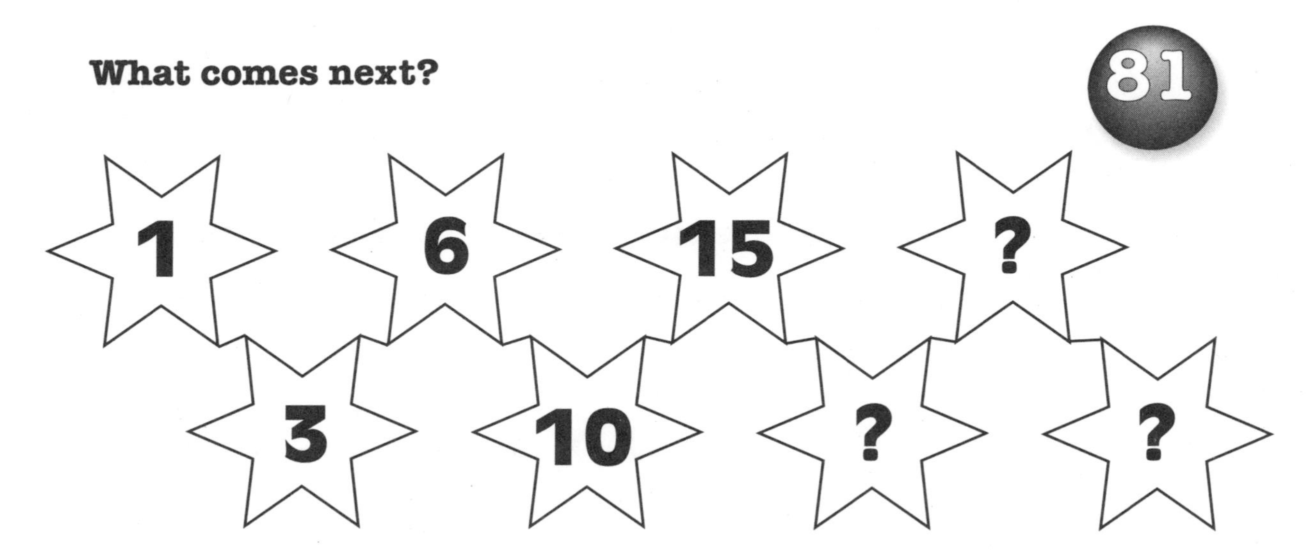

Describe the pattern in words.

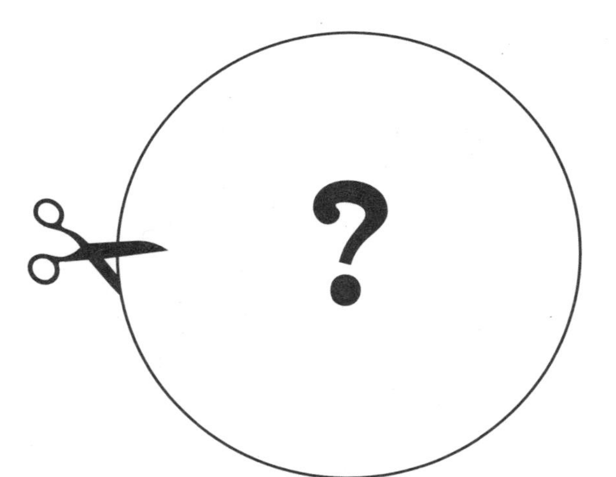

How many different ways can you cut a circle in half?

Explain.

©Addison Wesley Longman, Inc./Published by Dale Seymour Publications®

Deanna wrote clues about her address.

Use the clues. Find the number.

Clues

- $b = 36 \div 9$
- $b \times a = b$
- $d + b = 10$
- $d - b = c$
- $c - c = e$

Make up clues for your address or telephone number.

Give them to a friend to solve.

84

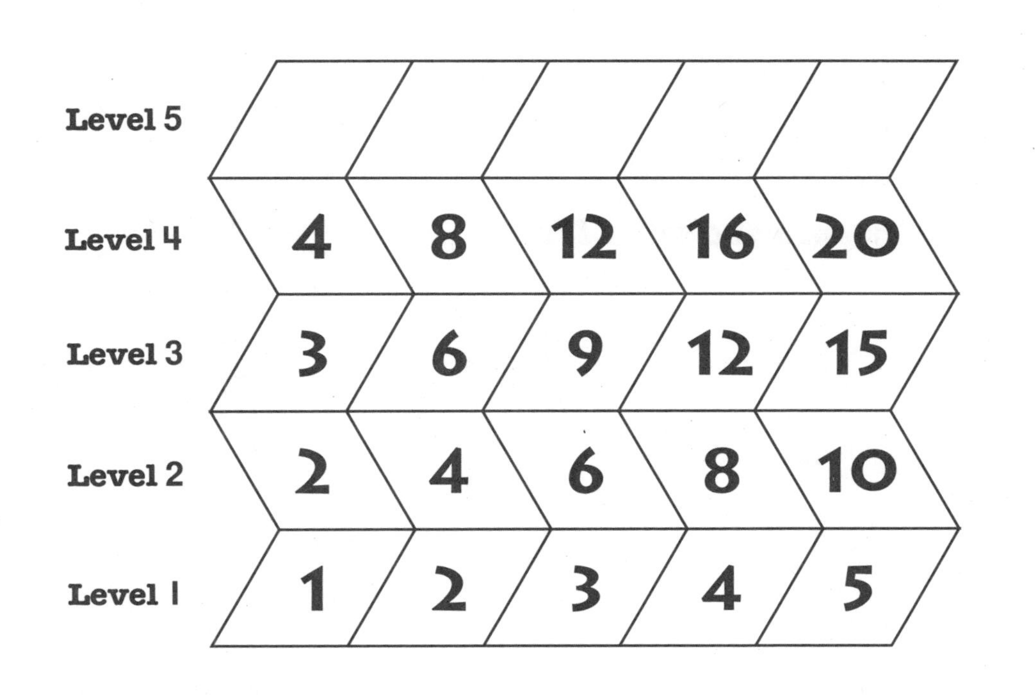

Level 5					
Level 4	4	8	12	16	20
Level 3	3	6	9	12	15
Level 2	2	4	6	8	10
Level 1	1	2	3	4	5

The pattern continues.

Ask three questions about the pattern.

Answer your questions.

©Addison Wesley Longman, Inc./Published by Dale Seymour Publications®

What number comes next?

Describe the pattern.

Make a new number pattern.

Have a friend describe your pattern.

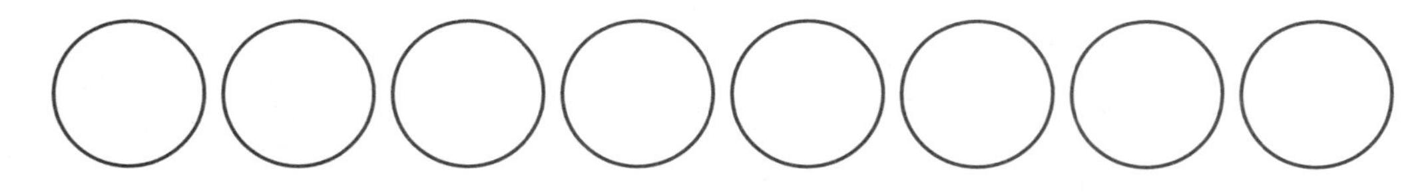

86

You are thinking of 39.

You want a friend to figure out your number.

Write a fourth clue so your friend can figure out your number.

Clues

- The number is less than 50.
- You say the number when you count by 3s.
- The number is greater than 30.
- ______________________________

  ____

87

Luis, Mario, and Rafael are brothers.

Each brother does not like a different vegetable: carrots, tomatoes, or eggplant.

Use the facts to tell which food each boy doesn't like.

Tell who is the youngest, in the middle, and the oldest.

Facts

- The oldest boy likes carrots.
- Luis does not like tomatoes, but an older brother does.
- Mario will eat eggplant but not carrots.
- Mario's younger brother also eats eggplant.

	youngest	middle	oldest
Name	______	______	______
Doesn't like	______	______	______

88

Kathy made a shape pattern.

The pattern continues.

Draw the 30th shape.

Tell how you decided what to draw.

89

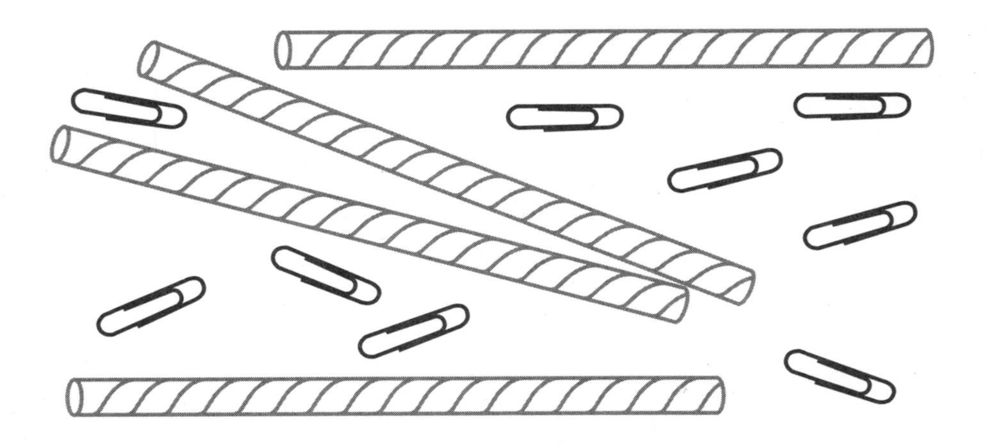

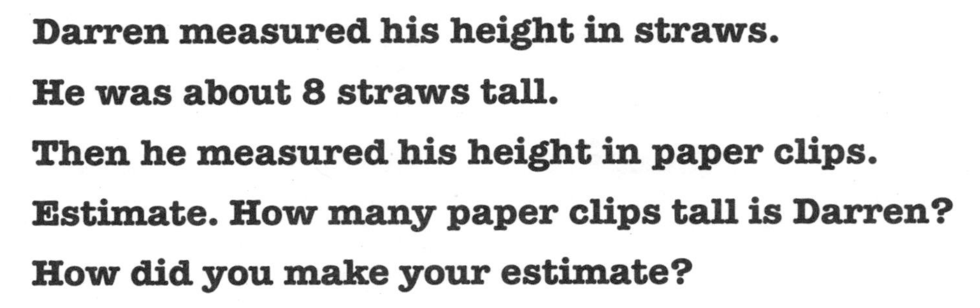

Darren measured his height in straws.

He was about 8 straws tall.

Then he measured his height in paper clips.

Estimate. How many paper clips tall is Darren?

How did you make your estimate?

90

Which would you rather have:

a 12-inch line of dimes

or

a 24-inch line of pennies?

Tell how you decided.

©Addison Wesley Longman, Inc./Published by Dale Seymour Publications®

The Home Now company builds apartment buildings.

The apartments are always side by side in a row.

Bushes are planted on the sides of the apartments.

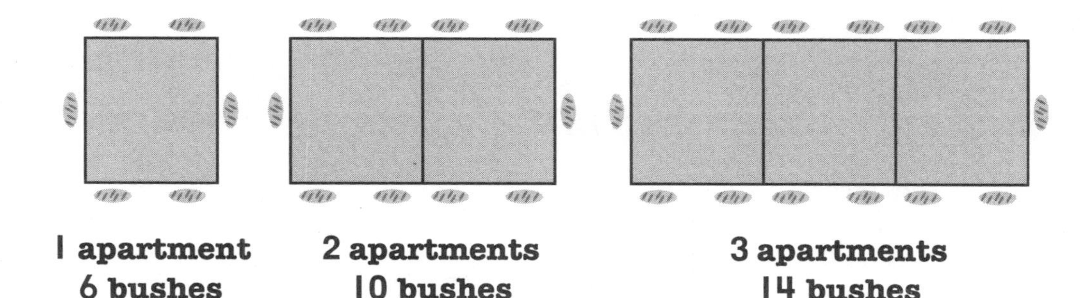

How many bushes will Home Now need for a building with 10 apartments?

How do you know?

Complete the rules.

Finish the tables.

A

Multiply by 3 and add 2.	
1	5
2	8
3	11
4	14
5	___
6	___

B

Multiply by ____ and subtract 2.	
1	1
2	4
3	7
4	10
5	___
6	___
___	28

C

Multiply by ____ and add ____.	
1	7
2	11
3	15
4	19
5	___
6	___

93

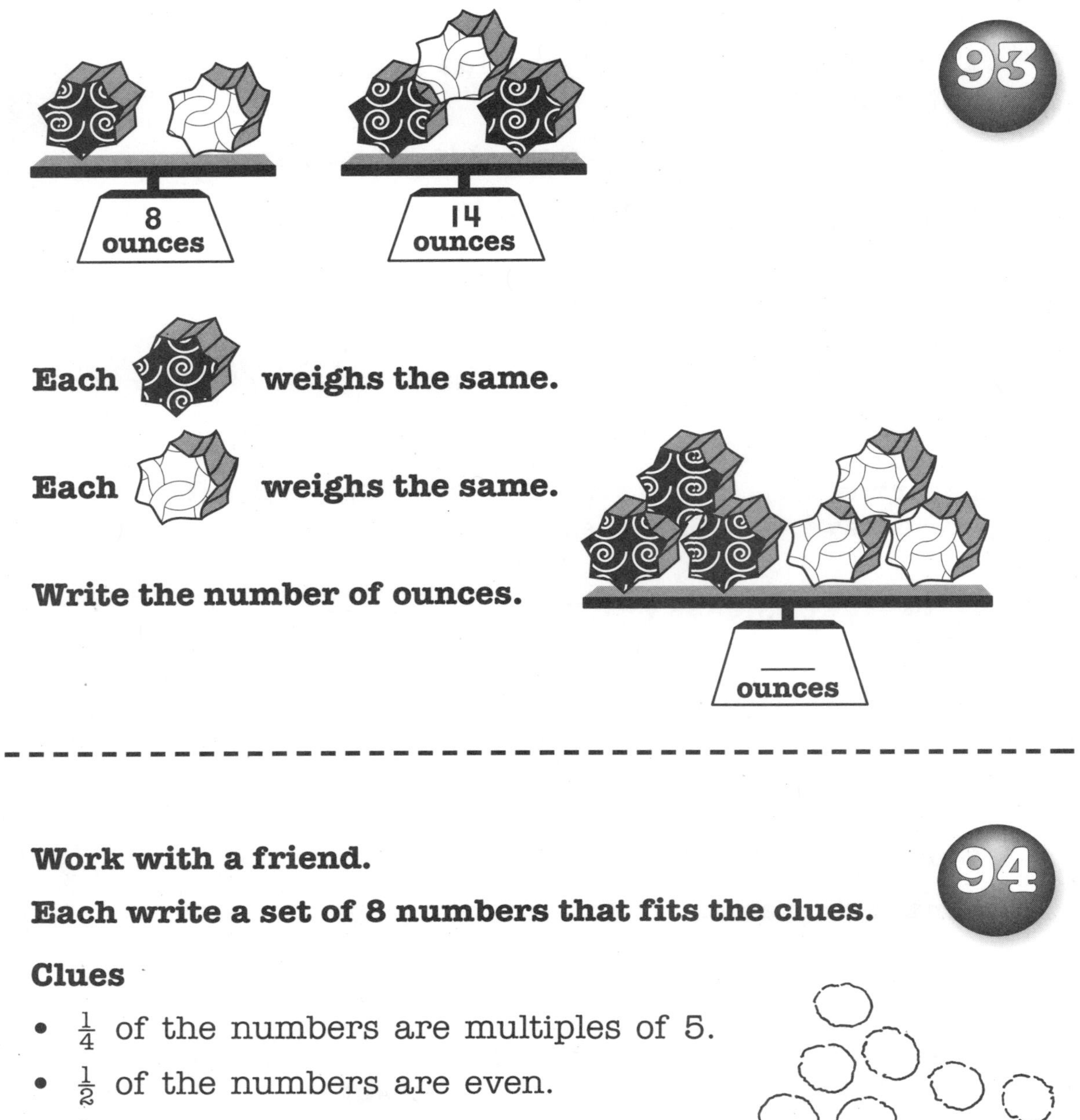

Each [dark shape] **weighs the same.**

Each [white shape] **weighs the same.**

Write the number of ounces.

94

Work with a friend.

Each write a set of 8 numbers that fits the clues.

Clues

- $\frac{1}{4}$ of the numbers are multiples of 5.
- $\frac{1}{2}$ of the numbers are even.
- $\frac{1}{2}$ of the numbers are less than 20.

Compare your answers.

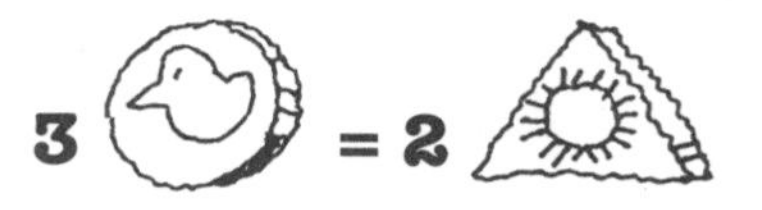

Which would you rather have:

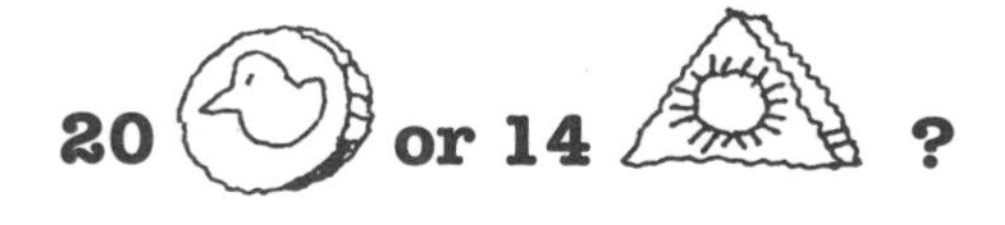

Why?

Write the correct numbers on the lines.

There are 20 cars.

Nine cars are blue and are not compacts.

Two cars are compacts and are not blue.

Three cars are blue compacts.

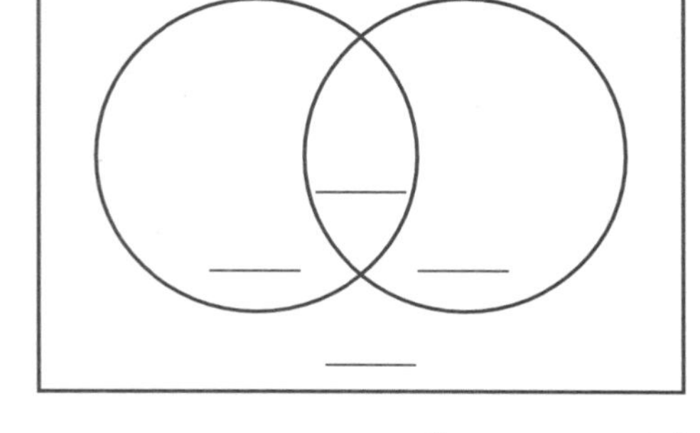

How many cars are not compacts and are not blue?

©Addison Wesley Longman, Inc./Published by Dale Seymour Publications®

97

The pumpkin is doing something special to these numbers.

Tell what the pumpkin is doing.

Solve these pumpkin problems.

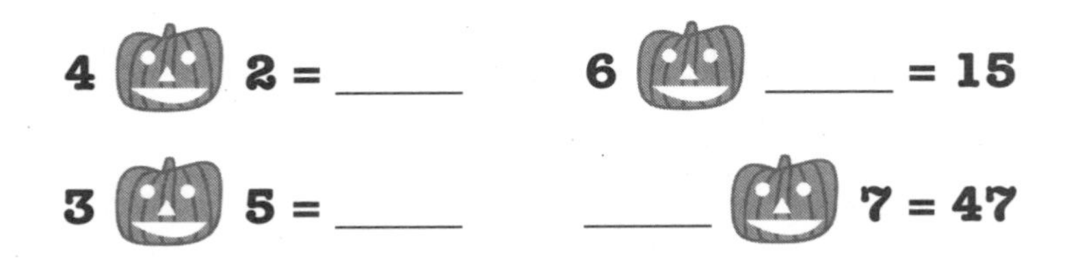

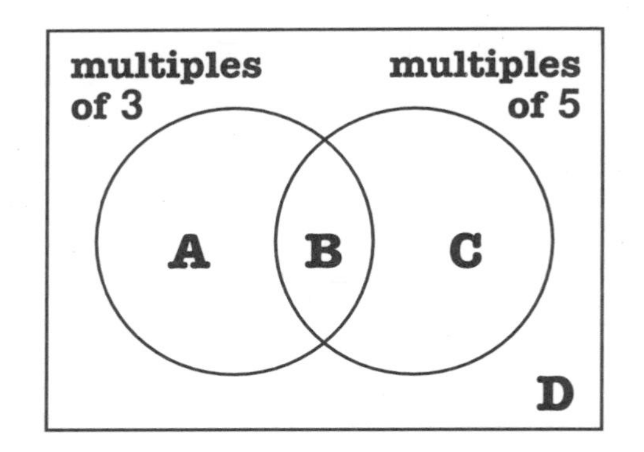

Tell two numbers that belong in each area.

Area A: ____ **and** ____

Area B: ____ **and** ____

Area C: ____ **and** ____

Area D: ____ **and** ____

Three of these are different views of the same cube.

One of these cubes is different.

Which cube is different?

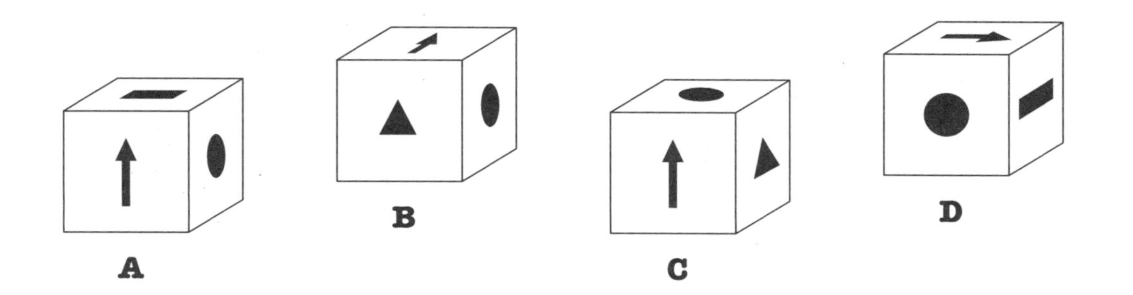

100

3 pints 5 pints

You want to measure 1 pint of lemonade.

You have only these two unmarked containers.

How can you use the two containers to get 1 pint of lemonade?

©Addison Wesley Longman, Inc./Published by Dale Seymour Publications®

Answers

1. Ken, 12; Danya, 7; Maria, 15; Brett, 10
2. Possible answers: A because every angle is the same. C because it has 3 sides. D because it is concave.
3. $8 + 10 = 18$, $10 + 12 = 22$; Possible patterns: An even number and the next even number are added. The sums differ by 4. The first (2, 4, 6, 8) and second (4, 6, 8, 10) addends are consecutive even integers. Each sum is 2 times the odd number between the even numbers being added.
4. Pattern Corner
5. Answers will vary.
7. 11; Explanations will vary.
8. from left to right: Kiran, Taylor, José, Mac, Carl
9. Answers will vary.
10. 1 quarter and 2 dimes
11. floor 8
12. Blake, flute; Amos, guitar; Larson, piano
13. Possible patterns: There are 2 numbers between consecutive yellow squares and 5 between consecutive blue squares. Every other yellow square is also blue. All blue squares are also yellow. After 3 rows, the color pattern repeats. Yellow squares run diagonally in one direction; blue squares run diagonally in both directions.
14. 16 pieces
15. Patterns will vary.
16. 9:20, gym; 10:00, math; 1:45, library; 2:30, art
17. Arrows alternate pointing up and to the right. Numbers in the third row and column are multiples of 3. The shape in the third column is a triangle; placement alternates from top left to top right. ▲ 9 ↑
18. B; It takes two A's to balance one B. A is half as heavy as B; B is twice as heavy as A.
19. no; A wide, short container, for example, could hold as much as a tall, thin one.
20. Answers must meet the conditions.
21. 2, 4, 6, 14, 20; 15
22. 10 9 8 7 6 5 4 3 2 1
    12 11 10 9 8 7 6 5 4 3 2 1
    20; 79
23. set 10: 10, 40; set 30: 30, 120
24. Vic, 64; Katie, 14; Daryl, 35; Ellen, 29
25. odd; odd; yes; Pairs of consecutive numbers always include one even and one odd, and even + odd = odd.
26. 17, 8, 5
27. Possible answer: All are even, > 17, and < 327. None are odd, 4 digits (or more), < 18, > 326, or multiples of 5. Some are multiples of 4, 2 digits, < 30, and > 30.
28. 5△ 15□ In building 20, there are 20 △ and 60 □.
29. O; ❀; Explanations will vary.
30. $5 + 5 = 10$, $6 + 6 = 12$, $7 + 7 = 14$, $8 + 8 = 16$, and $9 + 9 = 18$; C is always 1; two 1-digit numbers cannot have a 2-digit sum > 18.

B is always even; the sum of two even or two odd numbers must be even.

31. 444 pages
32. row 20; 12; row 14; Explanations and questions will vary.
33. 9; Maggie and 3 children are in front of the middle child. There must also be 4 people behind the middle child.
34. 10, 13, 5, 7
35. 21 pencils; Explanations will vary.
36. $7 \times 9 + 1 = 8 \times 8$; $9 \times 11 + 1 = 10 \times 10$; Patterns will vary.
37. 19; Clues will vary.
38 118, 226, 334, 442, 550
39. W, Leah; X, Monika; Y, Alan; Z, Bakari
40. 31,589,200; 3,553,600; 1,171,100; 2,382,500
41. 15, 15, 30
42. Ages should make Alex the oldest and Stacy the youngest.
43. 18, 9
44. 7, 19, 20, 11, 33, 15, 42, 30
45. Matthew, golf; Molly, swimming; Paul, tennis
46. from lower left: Tami, Alex, Nathan, Hani
47. Friday; November
48. Answers will vary.
49. the ball; Possible explanation: If the matching weights are taken from both sides, 2 balls balance 3 boxes, so 1 ball equals $1\frac{1}{2}$ boxes.
50. 1 or 2 years old; Terry is 13 and is younger than Aleta and older than Brigitte, so Aleta must be 14 or 15 and Brigitte must be 2 or 1.
51. 5 striped, 16 white, 21 in all; Explanations will vary.
52. 10 games; Possible explanations: 5 girls play 4 others ($5 \times 4 = 20$), but this counts each girl playing each other girl twice. Or, Louisa plays the other 4 girls, Tracy plays the other 3, Chantel plays the other 2, and Tia plays Opal, for $4 + 3 + 2 + 1 = 10$.
53. 15¢, 30¢, 90¢, 135¢
54. 2541
55. 42 cubes; Explanations will vary.
56. Halle's pizza was larger than Jack's. One piece of Halle's pizza was larger than half of Jack's pizza.
57. C; C has a polygon outside, a circle inside, and an odd number in the circle.
58. The answer equals the starting number. Adding and subtracting the same amount (20) and multiplying and dividing by the same number has no effect.
59. row 10, column A; Possible explanations: All multiples of 4 are in column D. Divide by 4 to get the row number. Since 36 will be in row 9, 37 will be the first number in row 10.
60. from left: Johnson, Reagan, Kennedy, Bush, Clinton
61. 20, 40, 60, 80, 100
63. 90
64. 19, 31, 301; Explanations will vary.
65. 48; Explanations will vary.
66. Possible descriptions: The numbers are multiples of 4. Or, the difference between numbers is 4. The 26th number will be 104; explanations will vary.
67. W and Y; Two round or oval shapes and a rectangle are in a polygon.
68. 132; Explanations will vary.
69. 23 tables; Explanations will vary.
70. Doug, Eggie; Caleb, Dowser; Edward, Chow
71. 88, 96

72. rectangular prism; Facts will vary.

73. Possible explanations: Turn the figure 90° counterclockwise and flip it over the line that bisects the rectangle's longer sides. Or, turn it 90° clockwise and flip it over the line that bisects the shorter sides. (The motions can be done in either order.)

74. green, 50; yellow, 5; red, 5

75. 27 beads; Explanations will vary.

76. 19; Possible explanations: Add 2 for each successive row. Or, count to find the tenth odd number. Or, multiply the row number by 2 and then subtract 1. Students might also list all the numbers.

77. A, Jin Lee; B, Thomas; C, Delia; D, Eric

78. Danny, 60 steps; Tomas, 30 steps

79. Eva, mouse; Stef, parrot; Gia, dog

80. 8

81. 21, 28, 36; Possible explanations: The differences between consecutive numbers are the counting numbers starting with 2. Or, these are the sums of consecutive counting numbers: $1 = 1, 3 = 1 + 2, 6 = 1 + 2 + 3$.

82. an infinite number of ways; Any straight cut through the center will separate the circle into two halves.

83. 14260; Clues will vary

84. Answers will vary.

85. 34; Double the number, subtract 1, repeat. Patterns will vary.

86. Possible clue: The ones digit is 3 times the tens digit.

87. youngest to oldest: Luis, tomatoes; Mario, carrots; Rafael, eggplant

88. circle; The pattern repeats every 4 shapes, so the 28th is a triangle, the 29th is a square, and the 30th is a circle.

89. Estimates and explanations will vary.

90. the line of dimes; The line of pennies is twice as long, but a dime is not only smaller than a penny, but equal in value to 10 pennies.

91. 42 bushes; Possible explanation: There are 2 bushes in front and back of each apartment (20 + 20) and 1 at each end (40 + 1 + 1 = 42).

92. A: 17, 20; B: Multiply by 3 and subtract 2; 13, 16, 10; C: Multiply by 4 and add 3; 23, 27.

93. 24 ounces

94. Possible set: 6, 8, 13, 15, 20, 21, 22, 23

95. 14 ; Possible explanation: 14 is 7 groups of 2 or 7 groups of 3 . 7 groups of 3 is 21, and 21 > 20 .

96. Six cars are not compacts and are not blue.

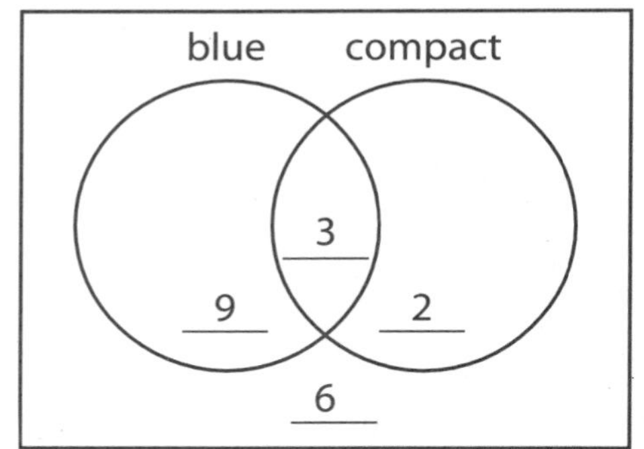

97. The pumpkin is doubling the first number and adding the result to the second number. 10, 3, 11, 20

98. Answers will vary.

99. C

100. Fill the 3-pint container and pour it into the 5-pint container. Fill the 3-pint container again. Use it to fill the 5-pint container, leaving 1 pint in the 3-pint container.

DETROIT PUBLIC LIBRARY
3 5674 05797442 1

W9-AED-771

The Whispering Town

For Will, Lizzy and Sophie. You are in my heart. Always and forever. – J.E.

To Giulia and the publisher who have always believed in me. – F.S.

KAR-BEN PUBLISHING
A division of Lerner Publishing Group, Inc.
241 First Avenue North
Minneapolis, MN 55401 USA
1-800-4-Karben

For reading levels and more information, look up this title at www.karben.com.

Library of Congress Cataloging-in-Publication Data

Elvgren, Jennifer Riesmeyer.
The whispering town / by Jennifer Elvgren ; illustrated by Fabio Santomauro.
pages cm
Summary: In Denmark during World War II, young Annet, her parents, and their neighbors help a Jewish family hide from Nazi soldiers until it is safe for them to leave Annet's basement.
ISBN 978-1-4677-1194-4 (lib. bdg. : alk. paper)
ISBN 978-1-4677-1196-8 (EB pdf)
1. Denmark—History—German occupation, 1940–1945—Juvenile fiction. 2. World War, 1939–1945—Denmark—Juvenile fiction. 3. Jews—Denmark—Juvenile fiction. [1. Denmark—History—German occupation, 1940–1945—Fiction. 2. World War, 1939–1945—Denmark—Fiction. 3. Jews—Denmark—Fiction.] I. Santomauro, Fabio, illustrator. II. Title.
PZ7.E543Whi 2014
[E]—dc23 2013002195

Manufactured in the United States of America
5-44263-13122-6/15/2017

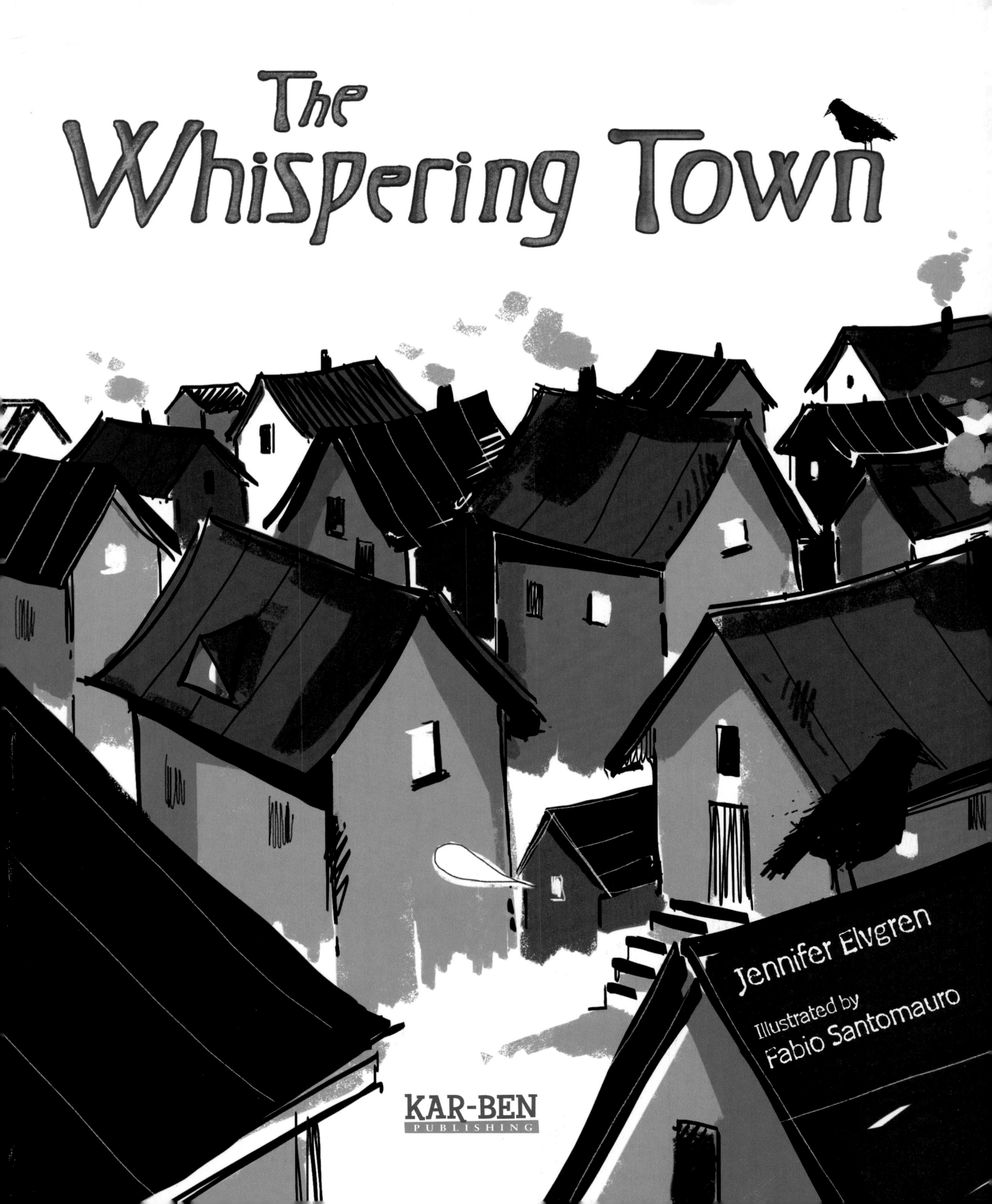
The Whispering Town
Jennifer Elvgren
Illustrated by
Fabio Santomauro
KAR-BEN
PUBLISHING

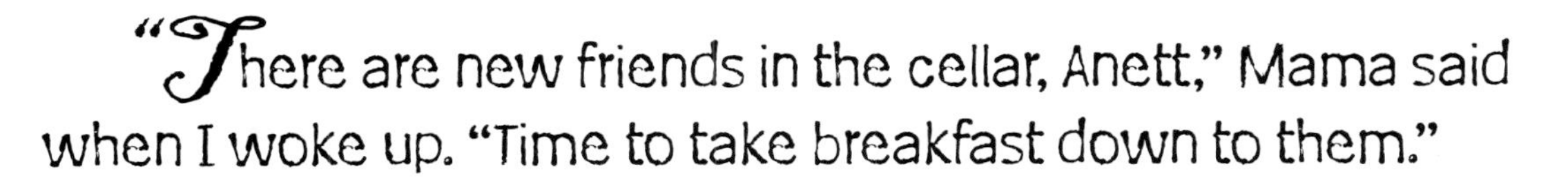

"There are new friends in the cellar, Anett," Mama said when I woke up. "Time to take breakfast down to them."

I paused at the top of the stairs. The cellar scared me because it was dark. But the whispering voices gave me courage.

When I reached the bottom, I entered the secret room where we hid Danish Jews from the Nazis. A woman and her son sat on a cot.

"I'm Anett," I said, holding out the basket. "Mama made you breakfast."

"I'm Carl." The boy took the basket and handed his mother a roll and a soft-boiled egg.

"We thank you," she said.

Back upstairs, I sat down to my own breakfast. "How long will our new friends stay?" I asked.

"Two nights," said Papa. "On the third night a boat will take them to Sweden."

"While they're here, we'll need more bread." Mama said.

After breakfast I walked to the bakery.

"We have new friends," I whispered to the baker.

"Here is extra," he whispered back, handing me a bulging bag. "Stay safe."

On the way home, I saw Nazi soldiers knock on a door across the street.

Even though they had been in my town for a long time, my stomach still knotted when I saw them.

“Mama, Papa, soldiers across the street!” I said when I came home.

Mama tapped three times on the cellar door to warn our friends to be quiet.

After the soldiers left, Papa looked up at the cloudy sky.

"No moon tonight," he said. "It will be difficult for our friends to find the harbor in the darkness."

The next day, I took food to the cellar again. Again I let the whispering voices guide me down the dark stairs.

“This will help the time pass,” I said, handing Carl some library books.

He took them and smiled. “I love to read.”

“Mama, I need new books,” I said, when I came upstairs.

After breakfast I walked to the library.

"We have new friends," I whispered to the librarian.

"Be careful," she whispered back, handing me extra books.

On the way home, I saw Nazi soldiers knock on our neighbor's door.

"Mama, Papa, soldiers next door!" I said when I came in the house.

Mama tapped three times on the cellar door.

After the soldiers left, Papa looked up at the cloudy sky.

"No moon again tonight," he said. "Maybe the clouds will clear tomorrow."

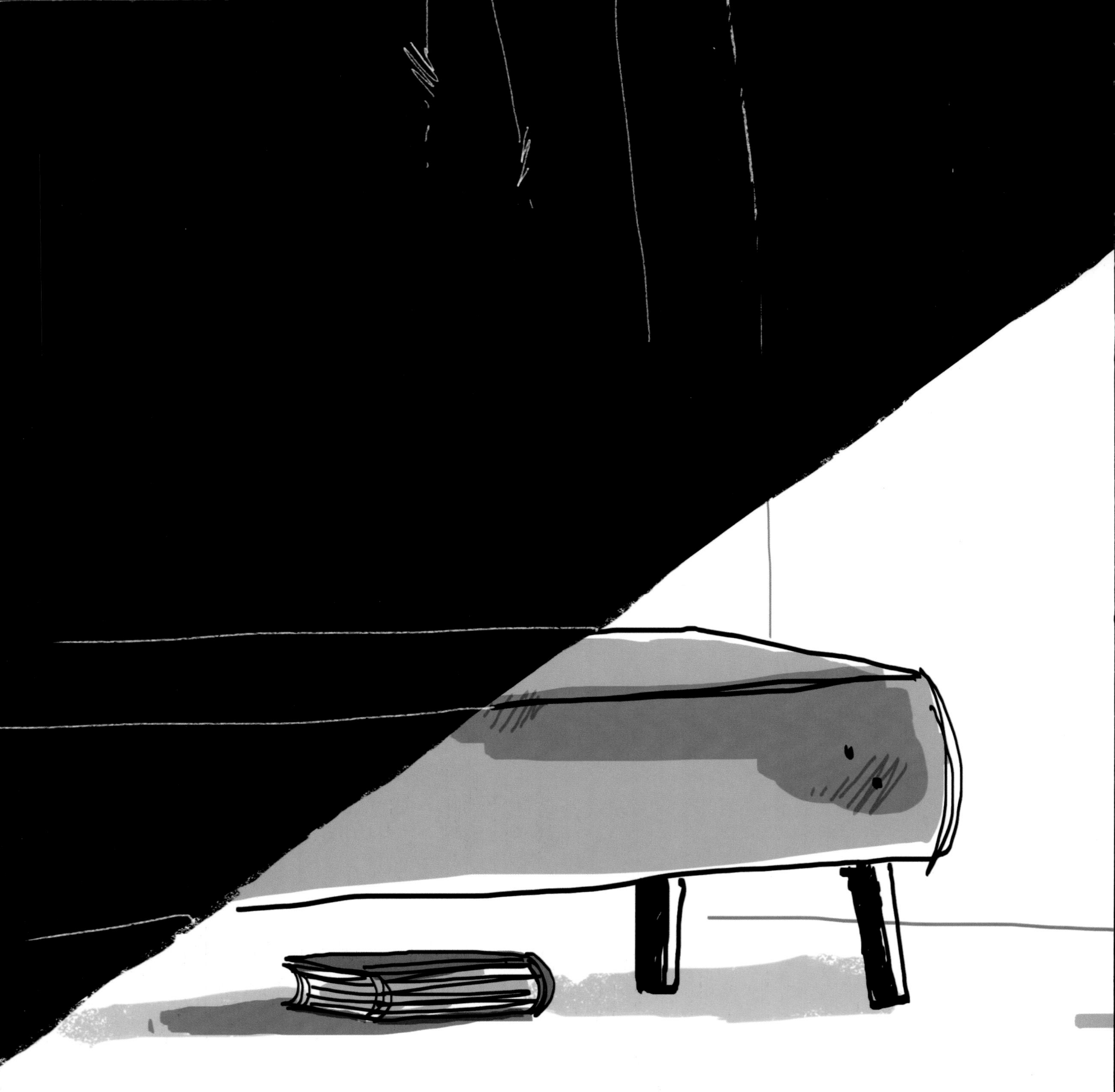

Again, the next morning, I let the whispering voices guide me down the dark stairs.

As Carl reached into the breakfast basket, a heart-shaped stone fell to the floor.

Carl picked it up. "I found this with my papa the last time we walked on the beach," he said.

"It's beautiful," I said.

"Anett, we need more eggs," Papa said, when we finished breakfast.

I walked to the farm.

"We have new friends," I whispered to the farmer.

"Wish them well," he whispered back, giving me extra eggs.

On my way home, I saw Nazi soldiers heading for our house. I cut across the alley and raced through our back door.

"Mama! Papa! The soldiers are coming to our house!"

They didn't answer me. No one was home.

I tapped three times on the cellar door.

Then I heard pounding on the front door.

"BOOM. BOOM. BOOM."

I opened it a crack.

"We've heard rumors that someone is hiding Jews on this street," said a soldier, pushing the door open.

"I haven't heard any rumors," I said, trying to stop my voice from shaking.

"When we find them, we will arrest everyone," warned the other soldier.

Trembling, I closed the door.

"The soldiers were here," I said, when Mama and Papa returned. "They are looking for hidden Jews."

"Brave Anett!" Papa hugged me. "Our friends must leave tonight even though it is cloudy. How can we get them safely to the harbor?"

I thought about being afraid of the dark cellar, and how the whispering voices guided me down the stairs.

"Papa, what if people stood in their doorways and used their voices to guide our friends to the boat?" I suggested.

Papa stood quietly, considering my idea.

"That might work," he said. "Help me to arrange it."

I ran to the baker , the librarian , and the farmer to tell them about our plan. They agreed to help spread the word around the village.

THIS
W
A Y

At midnight, Carl and his mama came up from the cellar. Carl pressed the heart-shaped stone into my hand. "Remember me always, Anett."

I held the little heart against my own.

After Carl and his mama slipped into the night, I leaned as far as I could out my bedroom window.

I heard our neighbor whisper from his doorway. "This way," he said, guiding Carl and his mother toward the harbor.

Then our neighbor's neighbor whispered, "This way."

The whispers continued from neighbor to neighbor, until Carl and his mama had safely reached the boat.

I squeezed the stone in my hand and imagined them walking free on the beach in Sweden.

AUTHOR'S NOTE

Less than a year after World War II began, Germany invaded Denmark. It would serve as a "buffer" to protect Germany from British attacks. Adolf Hitler also wanted the country's fertile farmland.

At first, the Germans allowed the Danish government to continue ruling. But as time passed, the Danes grew tired of the Nazis and began to sabotage the occupation.

By 1943, the Nazis could no longer ignore the Danish resistance and took over the government. Shortly after, they began to round up the estimated 8,000 Danish Jews and send them to concentration camps.

Danes hid Jews in private homes, warehouses, barns, hotels, and churches. Then they secured boats and hired fishermen to transport them across the sound to nearby neutral Sweden. Almost all of the Jews were smuggled out of Denmark.

About 1,700 Jews escaped from the small fishing village of Gilleleje. One moonless night, the town's citizens stood in their doorways and whispered directions to the harbor.